Massachusetts Town Greens

# MASSACHUSETTS TOWN GREENS

## A History of the State's Common Centers

ERIC HURWITZ

Globe
Pequot

Guilford, Connecticut

# Globe Pequot

An imprint of Rowman & Littlefield

Distributed by NATIONAL BOOK NETWORK

British Library Cataloguing in Publication Information Available

**Library of Congress Cataloging-in-Publication Data**

Names: Hurwitz, Eric, 1962- author.
Title: Massachusetts town greens : a history of the state's common centers / Eric Hurwitz.
Description: Guilford, Connecticut : Globe, [2016] | Includes bibliographical references.
Identifiers: LCCN 2015044889 (print) | LCCN 2015047520 (ebook) | ISBN 9781493019274 (pbk.) | ISBN 9781493019281 (ebook)
Subjects: LCSH: Historic districts—Massachusetts—History. | Commons—Massachusetts—History. | Parks—Massachusetts—History. | Public spaces—Massachusetts—History. | Massachusetts—History.
Classification: LCC F65 .H87 2016 (print) | LCC F65 (ebook) | DDC 974.4—dc23 LC record available at http://lccn.loc.gov/2015044889

# Contents

# CONTENTS

# CONTENTS

# *Acknowledgments*

Thanks to the local and state historians, the historical societies and commissions, and the many down-to-earth Massachusetts town, city and, village residents who have shared information and perspectives with me on the wonders of the Massachusetts town greens. Without their expertise and passion on significantly historic Massachusetts town commons, this book would not have been possible. They truly carry on the tradition from their ancestors of knowing their town commons. Also, thanks to my editors Tracee Williams and Amy Lyons for entrusting me to take on this challenging, yet rewarding project. Thank you to my beautiful wife, Joan Hurwitz, who has unconditionally supported my writing this book, and for all her wonderful help, encouragement, and town green perspectives. She is a cancer survivor, and I am so glad that she has recovered so well. For that and many other reasons, I am dedicating this book to Joan as she reflects the inner and external beauty of a beautiful Massachusetts town green! This book is also dedicated to our daughters, Emily and Katie, for being such great young citizens and acting as advanced editorial consultants with this book. Thanks to my parents, Leslie and Janet Hurwitz; Uncle Connie; the entire Hurwitz and Kerrigan families; and incredible friends from our hometown and well beyond—like the Smirk and Graham families—who have constantly encouraged me to write *Massachusetts Town Greens*. Additionally I would like to mention my childhood as the foundation for my interest in local travel, including town greens. My parents and I, along with my brother Marc, would often embark on "mystery rides" in our phony wood-paneled Ford LTD and Mercury Marquis station wagons, and, as a family, discover the fabulous Massachusetts back roads, scenic highways, and well-known communities. What great memories and a precursor that would eventually lead to discovering Massachusetts town greens!

The grass always seems greener on Massachusetts town greens.

Centrally located in most Massachusetts towns and cities, town greens have, since the seventeenth century, reflected cultural, religious, economic, and political factors within a community's evolution that are far more complex than the facade of a simple green parcel of land. Unique stories reside in virtually every marker, monument, memorial, bandstand, fountain, and pathway, as well as in the wise old trees that sometimes clearly go beyond simply providing scenery and shade. These town green fundamentals would have no stories, however, if not for the locals who have lived through the joys and sorrows, the victories and road bumps of everyday town life through what seems like an unbroken chain of significantly historic times now in its fifth century.

If life begins biologically through conception, then a community's seed evolves from a historically fertile Massachusetts town green ground—including the Puritan's community-based proprietary lands in the Plymouth area and their quest for independence from Britain in the 1775 Battles of Lexington and Concord during the American Revolution. That is why the grass always seems greener on a Massachusetts town green, as neighbors, in an inherently strong collective New England spirit, have always found hope, freedom, progress, and resolution even through the toughest times.

Ultimately, the Massachusetts town green has served as the barometer of a community's overall wellness. From the expansive grounds of the Boston Common to the Boston Post Road—America's first mail route dating back to 1673—national treasures in the form of local town greens indeed add a collective sense of community statewide.

"This is the physical and philosophical center of this place we call home," says Jack Authelet, a Foxborough, Massachusetts, historian. "We have been drawn here time and time again by the sense of community that unites us as we raise our voices in song, join our hearts in prayer, honor those who have served our town and country, and reach out to those who have turned to us in their hour of need."

**The West Brookfield Common is located on the famous Boston Post Road.**

Massachusetts town greens—often called town commons and sometimes village greens—have clearly possessed a community gathering place presence built within a New Englander's DNA through distinct evolutions. The meetinghouse lot served as the primary town green destination—when the Congregational Church predominantly controlled town government until the late 1700s and early 1800s. Agricultural fields existed on the outskirts of town, with town common lots centered on cemeteries, militia training fields, main roads, and common agricultural lands.

In 1833, the official separation of church and state in Massachusetts occurred, thus shifting the church to municipalities, according to *Terra Firma*'s "Common Wealth: The Past and Future of Towns Commons" (*Terra Firma* is a publication of the Massachusetts Department of Conservation and Recreation's Historic Landscape Preservation Initiative). This transformation resulted in agriculture and religion taking a back seat to "primarily social, political and civic uses where public assembly was often a primary event." Inns, taverns, and blacksmith shops became staples around the town common, along with eventually many other commercial and industrial endeavors born as roadways increased and the Industrial Revolution evolved.

While many envision the town commons back then as quaint and attractive, nothing could be further from the truth in many cases. Think of animals roaming the land—and the troughs, hay piles, animal pounds, horse sheds, and a certain unappealing byproduct that go along with them. With the exception of the expansive Boston Common and a few other large town greens, an animal presence didn't seem compatible with many of the smaller town parcels and only lasted briefly, if at all. Additionally, some town greens were built on flood plains, and it took landscape experts like the famous Fredrick Law Olmsted (he had many talents beyond just landscaping) to alleviate the issues. Going back even further, seventeenth-century settlers were not exactly focused on town green beautifications, instead more focused on preventing Indian attacks.

Fortunately, town green beautification projects amped up significantly between 1840 and 1880, when the Village Improvement Movement spearheaded a move toward better landscaped park grounds—fences, improved pathways, graded soil, planted grass, and lots of elm trees—with a vision toward maintaining and improving public spaces. While today you'll see things that weren't there "back in the day," like bandstands, ball fields, swimming pools, tennis courts, memorializations, fountains, lighting, and other modern elements, town greens still can vary greatly by town and city.

"There is no single use for commons today, no uniform appearance, any more than there was three centuries ago," John Stilgoe was quoted as saying in the "Common Wealth: The Past and Future of Towns Commons" report.

As the Robert and Lois Orchard Professor in the History of Landscape at the Visual and Environmental Studies Department of Harvard University, Stilgoe added, "But commons remain a part of New England life, still at the heart of many communities, often revealing in their appearance and uses the people's covenant with their shared space."

Today some Massachusetts town commons have added enhancements when framed by a church with a tall white steeple and historic homes and buildings. Some prefer town greens with a combination of green spaces, walkability, and adjacent local businesses, as best experienced in towns and cities like Boston, Lexington, Concord, Salem, Natick, Norwood, Bridgewater, Walpole, Taunton, and Wakefield, to name a few. Many Massachusetts town greens, however, have little to no shops or restaurants surrounding them, cases in point, Princeton, Brookfield, Hardwick, Shirley, Royalston, and Wendell. The lack of anything to do, however, can be advantageous in these smaller communities, as the town green concept is fully realized—townsfolk and visitors have no distractions, thus often fostering greater conversations and focus on events and observances at hand.

Going a step further, Dana offers nothing but a town green, save extant foundations and cellar holes, granite steps, fragments of paving, stone fence posts, walls, and a metal safe too big and heavy to relocate. You see, the Commonwealth of Massachusetts acquired Dana in the 1930s so that the Quabbin Reservoir could be created to eventually become the largest source of state drinking water. It is, essentially, a "lost village."

Dana aside, town greens have been gaining more popularity as people have returned to enjoying the simpler things in life. As families find it harder to justify paying high admission prices for popular travel attractions on full tanks of gasoline, they tap into their own community's resources—in this case, the town green—to enjoy free activities and connecting with their fellow neighbors. There's little cost in having a picnic, taking in a community day or farmers' market, listening to a summer concert, enjoying fall foliage festivals, or sitting on a bench to slow down the pace and revive the lost art of conversation.

A few years ago a family visiting from lively Virginia Beach, Virginia, attended a relaxed small town tree-lighting ceremony at a Massachusetts town green and immediately felt welcome by the community that shared their love of the holiday season. A town green beaming with holiday spirit like this has that incredible feeling, with some caroling, the count down to the light illuminating the tree, free hot chocolate and donuts for warming up, and surrounding businesses lending additional ambiance with candles in the windows and white lights on the storefronts. The night, in this case, was typical New England cold, but the feeling was so warm with the modern world put on hold in lieu of a good old-fashioned holiday event that very well could have been held more than a one hundred years ago. Some things are just timeless, and there's overwhelming evidence, year after year, day after day, that many of them take place at the town greens in Massachusetts towns and cities.

The pace of life in Massachusetts has increased so greatly in the past twenty years that many people have started to reject the superficial and material elements of suburban and urban ways of life in search of something more meaningful. For all the social media that's out there, as an example, the irony is that it can create antisocial situations and feelings of isolation, where the user is so tethered to technology that human interaction takes a back seat. Shopping malls and open-air centers might provide all the retail items one could ever hope for, but chances are you will never see anyone you know there—and if you do, the mission of the visit is to shop and buy, not stop and talk for a while.

The Massachusetts town green can serve as an antidote to this materialistic way of life. In towns and cities where stores and restaurants surround the town greens, one can have the best of both worlds—that is, using the town common as an idyllic meeting place for a picnic, town event, or walk, and then strolling across the street for some food and retail shopping. This type of layout also lends a one-of-a-kind experience: Unlike shopping centers that tend to all look the same or perhaps be too cold and sterile, each Massachusetts town has a look unlike any other. Assonet Village looks nothing like Bridgewater, and Bridgewater looks nothing like Williamstown, and Williamstown looks nothing like Petersham, and so on and so on. Some town greens are quite unusual looking, in fact: The Eastham town green has a windmill, Wakefield a beautiful lake, and Hopkinton a statue dedicated to a man who started the Boston Marathon for many years—the Hopkinton town common has been the starting point for this famous road race since 1924! 

How many town greens are there in Massachusetts? The Massachusetts Cultural Resource Information System shows 169 results online that also include individual parts of town commons listed (fences, paths, bandstands, and so on), so it's hard to say. The database does not include newer town commons like the one in Bellingham, as well as more traditional town greens such as in Norfolk, Pittsfield, and Bradford (part of Haverhill). We'll go with a general observance then: There are plenty of town greens to choose from in every Massachusetts county; communities without having any are exceptions!

With people rediscovering Massachusetts town greens, can these commons continue to exist in a state with rampant commercial, industrial, residential, and recreational development? Peter Stopt, preservation planner for the Massachusetts Historical Association, believes so.

"I do believe people are most aware of their town commons and if you ask them what they value most, it's going to be their town commons and civic buildings," said Stopt. "The National Register of Historic Places is more honorary offering less protection, but local historic districts look after their town commons and have more teeth in its protection."

Town greens are here to stay, so the question is, "How can we find out where to discover them?" Travel guides generally fail to tell readers about town greens in Massachusetts unless they are of extraordinary historical significance (like in Concord, Lexington, and Boston). While the lack of mention is unfortunate, the upside is that you generally won't have to deal with crowds as, generally, a Massachusetts town green will feel like your own discovery. There's undeniable empowerment in finding one's own travel place—or, for a resident, to tap into a local treasure—so do not be skeptical if a town green doesn't get mentioned through the travel guides or mainstream media. Back in the day when there was no 24/7 media the way we know it today—or travel guides, for that matter—word of mouth worked best to let people know about special places. Consider this book your word-of-mouth resource for Massachusetts town greens; these special places are New England's original "top travel attractions!"

With all that in mind, let's start our fun and educational tour of many of the historically significant town greens in Massachusetts!

# AMHERST

A classic college town, Amherst is home to the University of Massachusetts–Amherst, Hampshire College, and Amherst College—and a town common that earns high honors with its wonderful presence as a beautiful oasis in a bustling downtown district.

The town common actually comprises two parcels of land—a small traditional kind with benches and paved walkways hugging the retail district, and a long green space surrounded by old churches, Amherst College, and historic buildings like the Lord Jeffery Inn. While the smaller green is more populated due to its proximity to the core of the downtown area and its benches, the larger green catches the visitor's eye with its expansive parklike grounds—so increasingly rare in Massachusetts towns with higher populations.

Both town greens are simply stunning and look a lot different than they did in the mid-1800s, when the lands were nothing more than unkempt hay meadows—quite a contrast to a progressively thriving central district. Fortunately, the Ornamental Tree Association started the beautification of the town commons in 1853. It's interesting to note that William Austin Dickinson—brother of noted poet and Amherst resident Emily Dickinson—was the secretary of the Ornamental Tree Association, according to the Emily Dickinson website (www.emilydickinsonmuseum.org/). The Emily Dickinson homestead sits just a few hundred yards from the town green.

The Village Improvement Association picked up where the Ornamental Tree Association left off by transforming the "meadow into a civilized town common and imposed regulations designed to maintain a clean town center," according to the Emily Dickinson Museum

**Historic buildings and locally owned shops juxtapose wonderfully with the Amherst town green.**

website. The Dickinson website also states, "They added a tiered water fountain and ornamental fencing, planted elm trees, and filled in a frog pond. They also forced the Cattle Show, one of the town's most popular annual events, to another location because the cows damaged the grass. The common hosted military practices, commencement celebrations, bonfires, and touring circuses, including the Van Amburgh Circus, considered the "greatest circus in the world."

Today, academic types often sit on benches with their cups of coffee and laptops to catch up on the world, lesson plans, and homework. The town greens also serve as the perfect segue to the spacious grounds of Amherst College across the street, where students and visiting parents can enjoy long walks to and from the college and the two commons en route to a very impressive walkable downtown.

Notable events include the annual Cultural Survival Bazaar—usually held on Columbus Day weekend in October—featuring arts, music, and culture from around the world. The annual Amherst Sustainability Festival typically takes place the third Saturday in April with a dedication to preserving the agriculture and other natural resources of Amherst. The festival typically features stage performers, demonstration areas, animal displays, and recycling information.

After nearly forty-five years, the Amherst Farmers' Market remains a popular spring and summer town green attraction for local food, fun, and community—bringing in up to fifteen hundred visitors per market. Also popular is the annual Merry Maple Celebration that usually occurs during the first weekend of December with the lighting of a town green maple tree, plus band music, a parade, and Santa's arrival.

"It's like a party," says Amherst Farmers' Market Manager Tammy Toad Ryan. "Our market is in the parking lot between the north and south commons, and sometimes I'll walk from the farmers' market to see what's going on. There's really a lot going on and such a diversity of life. There are people passing out petitions, talking about politics, dancing . . . Even in the winter, you'll see lots of people enjoying the common, building snowmen. It's the heartbeat of the community."

The town greens help contribute to Amherst's small town look despite the population at around thirty-seven thousand—making it the largest town in Hampshire County. Many larger Massachusetts towns possess this contrast, where once off the beaten path in and around a town green, the community's personality gets quiet and often scenic in a hurry.

Originally inhabited in 1658 by the Umpanchla, Quonquont, and Chickwalopp tribes, settled by the English in 1727, and established as a township in 1759, the colonial governor assigned the town's name after Jeffery Amherst, 1st Baron Amherst—a hero of the French and Indian War. He was also a controversial figure as history goes back and forth on whether he was on the American or British side during the Revolutionary War.

Today, Amherst wonderfully embodies a historic leafy college town with well-preserved agricultural elements outside of town. It's an appealing mix with a town green that brings the best of both worlds to locals and visitors—that is, a rural space that connects to academia, myriad shops, restaurants, and service-oriented businesses within virtually seconds.

# ASSONET (FREETOWN)

Driving onto exit 10—less than a mile off the often-congested, modern commuter nightmare known as Route 24—leads to a wonderfully sleepy section of Freetown known as Assonet. With an unassuming variety store named Grampy's, the Assonet Inn restaurant that serves comfort foods like hot dogs and beans and pizza within a grand Victorian home, and the Eagle Trading Company that sells only cookbooks, Assonet is, otherwise, residential with some grand Colonial and Victorian homes on narrow streets. Recently visiting the 1880 Town Hall to ask for directions to the town green, employees seemed simultaneously shocked and pleased that someone from out of town came in to say hello. This is truly a "so quiet, you could hear a pin drop" village. One of the employees told me that there's "not much to do in Assonet," but "people who live here love it."

After getting directions to the town common—just 100 yards down the road—my sense was that there was something more to this initially bland-looking green. Walking the town common ultimately revealed a spaciousness that couldn't be noticed if just driving by, and the gazebo seemed as comfortable as an old shoe—imperfect but almost smiling at the world as one that couldn't be the prom queen but had a beauty of its own. Walking toward the back of the green revealed a pleasant view of the Assonet River and a sweet smell in the

**An early twentieth-century bandstand resides in the middle of the Assonet town common.**

air that seemed more rural New Hampshire than within ten minutes to urban Fall River.

The bandstand has an unusual history, as it was the original site of the Green Tavern in the early twentieth century. Boy Scouts would play in front of the tavern, but they lost their stage when the tavern was torn down. A local carpenter was paid twelve dollars a week to build the bandstand, thus putting the Boy Scouts' entertainment ambitions back in business and establishing a traditional New England staple that would become the anchor of the village green, according to the History Stands Still website Freetown page, http://bandstands .blogspot.com/search/label/Freetown%20MA.

While locals enjoy strolling the town common on a daily basis, this space truly comes alive every Father's Day with the Tuesday Club's Strawberry Festival featuring strawberry shortcake, hot dogs, lemonade, musical entertainment, and booths with local vendors. Proceeds go to deserving Freetown students looking to attend college. Many of those students, on their own, come back to help with the Strawberry Festival as an act of gratitude.

Established in 1987, the Strawberry Festival seems to bring out virtually the whole village.

"It (the town common during the Strawberry Festival) is a very busy place," said Cathy Oliveira, an organizer of the event. "The event started out small and has grown a lot, as it seems like we are out of space—exits 8 and 9 are all backed up and up to eighteen hundred people attend—still, it is a very comfortable space at the town common."

The population of Assonet is just over four thousand! Oliveira says that, in addition to local people, many from "Boston to Cape Cod to Rhode Island" come to the annual event.

Walking the village green somehow lends a historical aura that is validated by the village's interesting timeline. Established in 1659 and part of the Plymouth Colony until the Massachusetts Bay Colony merger in 1691, Assonet has a rich history that belies its small-town setting. The seventeenth century brought wars between English settlers and the local Wampanoag Indians, including King Philip's War. The eighteenth century saw Freetown become a fishing port, and the nineteenth century was an industrious period with railroads, ships, its position on the stagecoach and mail routes, and factories. Many of the factories closed in the twentieth century, and Freetown eventually evolved into a bedroom community for Taunton, Fall River, and New Bedford, as well as for patient commuters who drive forty miles into Boston. For many, Assonet seems like one of the last truly quiet suburbs in southeastern Massachusetts—or within the eastern United States industrial seaboard, for that matter. A good place to capture the village's relative refreshing silence is at the town green.

# ATTLEBORO

Attleboro once reigned as a major American jewelry manufacturing city, so prominently, in fact, that it was once known as the "jewelry capital of the world." That business jewel doesn't shine quite as much today, but Attleboro does have many other gems remaining—like the Attleboro Town Common.

The 1.3-acre town green aptly reflects the small city's big support of the US military with huge, prominent individual honor roll stones for those who paid the ultimate price during World War I, World War II, the Korean War, and the Vietnam War. The sites stand front and center in the minimally landscaped yet attractive town common that dates back to 1744. The sturdy obelisk monuments—tall, four-sided, narrow tapering structures ending in a pyramid-like top—look ready to battle against any type of harsh New England weather and truly reflect the strong nature of Attleboro soldiers who fought for our country's freedoms.

Tom Tullie, a retired Attleboro Veterans Department agent, speaks with great pride of how the dedication site evolved and how its permanence and main-attraction presence at the town green benefits Attleboro residents from all generations.

"I feel a permanency," says Tullie, of the site. "Before, they had a board with plexiglass. But this new site offers something enormous for vets, children, and grandchildren. Moms are out there walking with their babies, old-timers sit on benches. It just feels comfortable to be there and to know the dedication site will be there for a long time."

The project started in 1989 with dedication occurring in 1992. Tullie says that the initial $250,000 price tag for the project seemed

**Paying tribute to Attleboro residents who served plays a major role at the Attleboro city common—formally known as the Attleboro Veterans Memorial Common.**

"shocking," but contractors came forth asking, "How can we help?" Local residents donated, too, so the ultimate cost of the project was greatly reduced.

"I always thought Attleboro was a patriotic place," says Tullie, a retired US Navy veteran. "You can just feel that. Also, Attleboro has always been very politically active. I have never had a problem with the city council and mayor getting us what we need for projects and maintenance."

While downtown Attleboro has been undergoing an extensive, impressive revitalization, the city common—which has always served as the central district's only park—has remained virtually unchanged in its innately pleasing triangular appearance. Maple and oak trees grace the town common, as does the flagpole—erected in 1942—that honor Attleboro citizens in the armed forces.

Attleboro Mayor Kevin Dumas is a lifelong resident who appreciates the current version of the city common, as well as its revitalization in the early 1990s. "The common is a special place," says Dumas. "It's a place to congregate and has that strong military presence. It looks great, too, with good care put into the area—the embankment, flags flying, sod, irrigation."

Dumas remembers the city green as a child, but feels it looks best in its current version. "It was always a place to be respected, but the new area established by the vets is great. There was an undesirable element, but that transformed when the military community helped make this location a place of pride."

It's ironic that the town common was never used as a military training ground, given the city has traditionally been steeped in military pride and support. That military culture is so greatly respected in Attleboro that the town green is today known as the Attleboro Veterans Memorial Common.

Also interesting to note is that in 1995 the Second Congregational Church (built in 1748) tried to regain control of the town green land. According to *A Sketch of the History of Attleborough*, by John Daggett, the dispute was resolved by fifteen citizen committee members who decided that "the premises to be held forever for public purposes as a Park or Common . . ." Today the church towers high above the Town Common, creating a wonderful juxtaposition that surely says, "This is New England."

Interestingly, the Attleboro town common does not feature as many events as Capron Park—a beautiful thirty-acre park at 201 County Street that also features an eight-acre zoo. Capron Park holds most of the prominent community gatherings. As an appropriate decision, though, the Attleboro Veterans Day observance is held annually at the foot of the town common.

If by chance the town common is hard to find, just look for the huge landscaped letter A—carved from bushes. It really stands out, and it's a rarity among town commons in New England—that is, to have a landscaped first letter of a town's name at a town green. That carved letter, the town green, and the city, in general, definitely get an A for showing consistent community pride!

# BARRE

Barre is located geographically in the middle of the state, but there is nothing middling about the Barre Common Historic District.

With four contiguous town commons bounded roughly by South, Exchange, Main, Pleasant, Broad, School, and Grove Streets, the Barre Common District—which dates back to 1792—remains the central point of the town's civic life. Surrounded by many nineteenth-century buildings, beautiful white churches, and businesses including a theater and restaurants, the Barre town common from virtually all perspectives looks like the quintessential New England small town. The town commons feature several military dedication sites, a gazebo, a fountain, benches, and paved walkways and plenty of green grass.

The gazebo, in particular, stands out as a famous local attraction. Barre is known as "the band concert town of New England," with its three bandstands dating back to the 1880s. Townsfolk deemed the first bandstand's platform too high, and eventually replaced it with a safer, more modern second version. That bandstand lasted about forty years, until public sentiment favored a larger bandstand to meet the needs of a growing community.

The Barre Public Amusement Association formed a committee, chaired by Mr. Martin Smith, to discuss and initiate the building of a new and larger bandstand, according to the History Stands Still Barre web page (http://bandstands.blogspot.com/2009/04/barre-ma.html). Linda Payne, who compiled the information shown on that website, wrote that "the bandstand would be a memorial to Mr. G. Harding Allen, one of the most prominent citizens of Barre, who had died the previous autumn."

**A monument, a church, a fountain, and plenty of green grass help make the Barre town common a classic traditional New England destination.**

In the tradition of the past two Barre bandstands, locals funding the bandstand proved successful. According to Payne, "children of the town were urged to take part in the fund raising, contributing quarters, dimes, and nickels, which would demonstrate their youthful importance to the community and as a learning experience in carrying out community projects."

A Worcester company was hired to construct the bandstand, but only if Barre labor "be employed as far as possible." The commission also required that the stonework base "match the ornamental stonewall bordering the Allen Estate," which is nearby and within view across the street, states Payne.

The new bandstand debuted in July 1931 and, as Payne writes, "became the new centerpiece of the common with August 6th marking the dedication in memory of Harding Allen."

Payne says that the celebration of the new bandstand resulted in "automobiles . . . being parked in 'best-view' places all around the common. The estimation by the beginning of the ceremonies was that over 2,000 cars were lined up on every street leading into town."

Of course a rousing concert took place that day, courtesy of the famous Worcester Brass Band. Payne adds that all agreed that this fine new structure was a great example of "achievement through cooperation."

And band concerts continue to this very day on a very beautiful bandstand!

Margaret Marshall, a local historian, says that the town common in the early 1800s was known for its fairs, but unfortunately that came to end when a man complained about not being able to cross the street due to "horses all over the place." Marshall adds that in the early 1900s, Barre took on almost a vacation retreat appeal "until the railroad came and people were able to travel to different places." A hotel stood proudly at the town common, providing the perfect small town New England look with great views of the common. That hotel building remained until the early 1990s, when a fire ruined the building.

Marshall says that a renovation project around the town green started in summer 2015 to rectify a rather hectic traffic pattern, but would in no way compromise the integrity of the common. Regardless, locals love their Barre town common.

"There is a sense of pride about it," says Marshall. "It has that colonial common look."

A short "101" on Barre history: The community was named after Isaac Barré, a member of the British Parliament who opposed the taxation of America. The town of Barre did not start out as the "Town of Barre." From the beginning of the earliest kept records, Barre was part of Rutland. The town was part of the Naquag grant and was made the "Northwest District of Rutland" in 1749. In 1774 the town incorporated and was called "Hutchinson." Two years later a petition for a different name resulted in it being called "Barre," with a population of 734. During the Industrial Revolution, it became known for its production of farming equipment and palm leaf hats.

With the village green as a former militia training ground and site of an animal pound, Barre today retains a wonderful sense of history (designated for listing on the National Register of Historic Places in 1976), yet has a foot in the twenty-first century, with its modest offerings of local businesses centered around the town common. 🌿

# BEDFORD

Bordered by historic Lexington and Concord, Bedford doesn't have the household name of those two historic communities, but as a town settled in 1642 and incorporated in 1729, it does have its share of significantly historic sites. The town green is a beauty to this very day and the site of the first (1729) and second (1816) meetinghouses, military training grounds, and town pound, schoolhouse (1741), and bell tower (1753).

The First Parish in Bedford—now a Unitarian Universalist church—stands as the most prominent structure on the town green (unlike most churches that are now located off the common). When Bedford became incorporated in 1729, locals did not want to take the journey to churches in Concord or Billerica, so they petitioned and requested permission to form their own church, according to the First Parish website (www.uubedford.org/about-us/heritage.html). The petition included this lament: "In the extreme difficult seasons of heat and cold we were ready to say of the Sabbath, 'Behold, what a weariness is it.'"

That is how the First Parish in Bedford at 75 Great Road became established. The original meetinghouse, badly damaged in the "great gale" of September 1815, was replaced by the present building in 1817, according to the First Parish in Bedford.

The First Parish in Bedford has had thirty-two senior ministers since 1730. The church notes that a pair of pews in the rear of the sanctuary were used in the first meetinghouse, with one having "1728" carved on its back. The stunningly beautiful steeple clock with its bell weights comprises a "wooden vertical shaft (that) is the arm of the pendulum that maintains the time. The brass wheel at the top of

The First Parish of Bedford sits on the attractive Bedford town green.

the pendulum is used to adjust accuracy of the clock by changing the length of the pendulum." Meneely Bell Co., Troy, New York, created the bell with an inscription that reads:

PRESENTED TO THE FIRST PARISH CHURCH UNITARIAN IN MEMORY OF GEORGE RICHARD BLINN BY HIS WIFE CLARA A BLINN 1886–1926. . . TO LIVE IN THE HEARTS WE LEAVE BEHIND IS NOT TO DIE.

During the steeple renovation of 1987, screening was installed in the belfry to reduce the pigeon problem that contributed to oxidation of the structure!

Located on the appropriately named Great Road, the town common area is not just about an attractive town green and the First Parish, however. The area, in fact, is nearly as impressive as Concord and Lexington's—noteworthy, given those two towns' important roles in American history—with its incredible collection of well-maintained old homes and churches. The busy roads in this district, quite honestly, do impede the history of the area—as Lexington and Concord are set up better for tourists—but don't ever let that deter you from visiting this wonderful area of Bedford. It's requisite New England and Massachusetts travel for those who have a love or interest in history. On Great Road where the town common is located, posts commemorate the march of the Bedford Minutemen on April 19, 1775, as they headed toward Concord at the start of the American Revolution, according to the Our Town Bedford Kids.com website (http://bedfordkids.com/our-town/).

Interestingly enough, the neat look of the town common has little resemblance to the previous version, which "in colonial times was larger in size and crisscrossed by unpaved, muddy tracks and dotted with puddles," according to the Bedford Historical Society website (www.bedfordmahistory.org). The "Old New England" look did not evolve until the mid-1800s.

In addition to the First Parish, the locally designated Bedford Historic District features the 1710 Kidder-Fitch Homestead (Tavern) at 12 Great Road, which is the oldest building in the town center, according to Freedom's Way website (www.freedomsway.org/towns/bedford/bedford.html). The Finch Homestead serves as the location where the Bedford Militia and Minutemen met for breakfast before their march to Concord on April 19, 1775.

Wilson Park, at the intersection of Great, North, and Concord Roads, sits just off the town common and has an interesting connection with the Fitch Homestead. Freedom's Way states that "after their breakfast at the Fitch Tavern, the Bedford Minutemen, under the command of Capt. Jonathan Wilson, mustered here in preparation for their march along Concord Road to meet the Bedford Militia at Merriam's Corner in Concord. An annual Pole Capping ceremony held each spring still honors Revolutionary resistance to tyranny."

Near the town common is the Old Burying Ground on Springs Road, Bedford's first cemetery with gravestones of approximately four hundred early citizens (of about fourteen hundred thought to be buried here), according to Freedom's Way. Forty-three Revolutionary War soldiers—including three former slaves—are interred here and memorialized on a plaque. The African Reservation in the northwest corner of the burial ground features slate gravestones, winged skulls, wreathed urns, and other funerary symbols, according to the Bedford Historical Society.

The Old Town Hall at 16 South Road is also a gem, an 1856 Italianate listed on the National Register of Historic Places. This site also served as a town office, school, jail, library, town meeting hall, and social hall during its various iterations.

Before leaving the Bedford town green area, be sure to visit the Bedford Free Public Library at 7 Mudge Way (very close to the common) where they have, on display, *The Bedford Flag*. The Bedford Public Library website (www.bedfordlibrary.net/town/bedford_flag.htm), describes this historical attraction as "The Bedford Flag is the oldest complete flag known to exist in the United States. It is celebrated as the flag carried by the Bedford Minuteman, Nathaniel Page, to the Concord Bridge on April 19, 1775, the beginning of the American Revolution, but it was already an antique on that day. It was made for a cavalry troop of the Massachusetts Bay militia early in the colonial struggle for the continent that we call 'the French and Indian Wars.'"

Bedford makes good use of its town green with many seasonal events, including the holiday tree lighting typically held the first week of December, the First Parish Plant and Craft Fair often on a Saturday in mid-May (see https://plantfair.wordpress.com for more info), and the First Parish Apple Festival that usually takes place on the last Saturday in September. 🍂

# BELCHERTOWN

If driving Route 121 north from the Mass Turnpike to the intersection in Belchertown center, make sure to take an immediate left. If not, you're missing one of the nicest town commons in Massachusetts.

Just beyond the small town parking lot lies a five-acre town green surrounded by churches, Colonial homes dating back two hundred years, and a few stores and offices. Originally called "Grasse Hill" as part of an original five-hundred-acre grant, the common size has been reduced greatly, but the presence of a well-established historical, governmental, and geographic center of town is still well intact. The Belchertown town common looks and feels like small town New England at its finest. It is wonderfully lined with trees that look especially beautiful in the fall with their brilliant foliage colors, and it has an unusual-looking bandstand and thoughtful memorials dedicated to those who have served.

Town greens often give us a clue about the personality of a town, and Belchertown is no exception. That pastoral, scenic town green reflects a quiet country town in the Pioneer Valley of western Massachusetts that prides itself on small businesses, farms, orchards, and a close-knit quality of life that has remained despite a consistent population growth into a mid-size town. While Belchertown sometimes feels like a suburb, the small town template can never be taken away—and that most prominently includes the town green as a traditional gathering place. Although this is where men mustered and drilled for the Revolutionary and Civil Wars, the Belchertown town greens have been known predominantly as a parklike destination for locals to enjoy. That neighborly togetherness can be best experienced at the Belchertown

The Belchertown town common looks great in the fall—or any other time of the year, for that matter.

Fair, which was established in 1856 as an agricultural event. Each year volunteers put in countless hours to create this three-day town-green event that is "a unique blend of history and community and free entertainment as well," according to the Belchertown Fair website (www.belchertownfair.com/2015/free-entertainment/). Highlights at this free-admission event—typically held in late September—include a parade, musical entertainment, an exhibit hall for local farmers and crafters, photographers and special interest groups, horse pulls and ox draws, and plenty of food vendors.

Belchertown's bandstand was created in 1878 "for the Farmers and Mechanics Club who were in charge of the Belchertown Fair held every October 12th," says the Belchertown bandstand history page on the History Stands Still website (http://bandstands.blogspot.com/2009/04/belchertown-ma.html).

Monuments include the Soldiers' Monument dedicated in 1885 and topped with a statue of a Civil War soldier. The monument reads:

DEDICATED TO THE MEMORY OF THOSE WHO
FOUGHT AND DIED
FROM THIS TOWN IN THE REBELLION 1861–1865
AND ALL SOLDIERS NOW
CITIZENS OF BELCHERTOWN.
ALSO TO THE MEMORY OF ALL THOSE FROM
BELCHERTOWN WHO SERVED
IN THE REVOLUTIONARY OR ANY COLONIAL OR
UNITED STATES WAR.

Belchertown, the second geographically largest town in the state at sixty square miles, was first inhabited by Indians, but then known for many years as Cowie's Spring and then Cold Spring before becoming incorporated as a town in 1761—named after territorial governor John Belcher, also one of the landowners in town. As the agriculture industry gave way to water-powered factories along the Swift River, Belchertown became well-known for its saw- and gristmills and paper, wool, shoddy, and cotton factories. Belchertown also became famous for its carriage, sleigh, and wagon industry, where "long convoys of carriages were taken south to Virginia, and orders came from as far away as Persia and Australia," according to the Belchertown Massachusetts website profile page (www.belchertown.org/residents/general _town_info/profile_of_belchertown.php).

Today the industries are largely long gone but, thankfully, none of the Belchertown Center Historic District—added to the National Register of Historic Places in 1982—has traveled that route. Nice preservation in an idyllic setting might serve as common characteristics for many Massachusetts town greens, but few rival the overall look of Belchertown. Whatever you do, don't drive straight through town and miss this town green gem!

# BOSTON

The Boston Common is the hub of Massachusetts town greens and the oldest park in the country, dating back to 1634. This fifty-acre park, in the heart of the city, possesses a remarkable history, as it has been used for many purposes throughout the years—some rather morbid like public hangings until 1817, and others intolerant like blacks not being allowed on the premises until July 4, 1836, according to the website History Stands Still: The Background of Bandstands Throughout New England (http://bandstands.blogspot.com).

Cattle grazed the Boston Common until 1830. In 1823, Boston officials enforced Boston Common rules that included allowing no one to graze more than one cow at a time. By 1830, cows were not permitted on the premises and had to "mooo-ve" (sorry for the bad pun).

According to History Stands Still: The Background of Bandstands Throughout New England, soon after this rejection of cows, amusements for the public became the main Boston Common attraction. Boston Common ways of life included serving as a launching site for balloon flights and an activities center for traveling entertainment shows, puppet shows, telescopes, scales, blowing machines, and booths selling gingerbread, spruce beer, lemonade, and sugar plums. The city incredulously set up a "Smokers Circle"—a place-to-be-seen spot for young women from the posh Beacon Hill neighborhood—astounding given the antismoking rules and regulations of modern-day Massachusetts.

Before that, though, the Boston Common served as a transitionary point for our country's history: British troops were stationed on the Boston Common before the American Revolution and deployed

**Boston Common is located in the heart of one of America's great cities.**

from this land to face resistance at Lexington and Concord in April of 1775.

Many famous people have spoken at the Boston Common, including Pope John Paul II, Martin Luther King Jr., and feminist leader Gloria Steinem, according to the City of Boston website. The late actress and singer Judy Garland (Dorothy in the legendary *Wizard of Oz* movie) gave her largest concert here in 1967 with one hundred thousand people in attendance.

The Parkman Bandstand, erected in 1912, is a revered attraction that has accommodated many entertainers performing for the public. The bandstand might just be as fascinating as those who have entertained here: It's a neo-classical structure that looks like a modified copy of the Temple d'Amour at the Petit Trianon, Versailles, France, and was built with pink Knoxville Marble, states the History Stands Still: The Background of Bandstands Throughout New England website. The bandstand is not used nearly as much as in the past, with just occasional concerts. It's now more of a historical icon and meeting place at the Boston Common.

Declared a US Historic National Landmark in 1987, the Boston Common extends far beyond its core location bounded by Tremont, Park, Beacon, Charles, and Boylston Streets. The Emerald Necklace, a seven-mile network of connected parks spanning the city's neighborhoods, offers twelve hundred acres of wonderful green space, including Franklin Park, the Arnold Arboretum and Jamaica Pond in Jamaica Plain, Olmsted Park, the Riverway, Back Bay Fens, and Commonwealth Avenue Mall and Boston Public Garden, according to the Emerald Necklace Conservancy website. The Boston Public Garden is located at the Boston Common and was the first public garden in the United States. Initially a space for the Victorians to display their love for gardening, the Boston Public Garden today features more than eighty species of plants and is home to the legendary Swan Boats on Boston (more on that later in this section), states the Boston Discovery Guide website.

Notable attractions on the main Boston Common land feature the Alexander Hamilton statue, 9/11 memorial, George Washington statue, *Make Way for Ducklings* statue, Central Burying Ground (final resting place for Revolutionary War soldiers and many more), Soldiers and Sailors Civil War Monument, Shaw Memorial, and Brewer Fountain.

Perhaps the most beloved Boston Common attraction is the Swan Boats of Boston, where pedal boats with inanimate swans have offered scenic summer rides around the lagoon since 1877. The Frog Pond is another wonderful Boston Common attraction featuring an idyllic location for public ice skating in the winter and a wading pool in the summer (the Tadpole playground and a carousel are nearby). Notable events include the Commonwealth Shakespeare Company's Shakespeare on the Common, Boston Lyric Opera's Outdoor Opera Series, lighting of the Boston Common Christmas Tree, and fireworks during Boston's First Night celebration on New Year's Eve.

The Boston Common is also the southern end starting point of the Freedom Trail, a free historic attraction focusing on the American Revolution. The free two-and-a-half-mile red-brick walkway through Boston neighborhoods includes historic meetinghouses, museums, and churches.

What's not located on the Boston Common makes the land all that much more special—that is, some of the significant historic buildings that surround it, including the Massachusetts State House, the Masonic Grand Lodge of Massachusetts, and Emerson College.

# BRADFORD (HAVERHILL)

Take a look around the Bradford Common and its Bradford Common Historic District, and you'll see something that doesn't fit in at all with the perceived image of Haverhill, a city known for its significant industrial roots.

Eighty-six historic homes create a remarkable walk down memory lane, including architectural styles like Greek Revival, Neo-Georgian, Colonial, Federal, Second Empire, Gothic Revival, Victorian, and Queen Anne Style. Add the Bradford Church of Christ, with its "newest" version dating back to 1848, and you have an encyclopedia of architectural styles that one Haverhill Society staffer, respectfully asking not to be identified, says, "is a mix that is second to none in Massachusetts."

Located on the north side of the town green is Kimball Tavern, an 1840 home once owned by Bradford Academy (more on that in a moment). The Don Orione property—with two Colonial Revival buildings with Arts and Crafts influence forming the estate-like setting—goes back to the early twentieth century as a religious retreat and summer camp for members of Don Orione congregations, according to Massachusetts Heritage Landscape Inventory Program's May 2005 "Haverhill Reconnaissance Report." Other locally famous historic homes include the 1836 Horatio Pearl House (Greek Revival), the 1849 Dr. Atwood House (Gothic Revival), the 1856 Hopkinton

**The Bradford Common provides a scenic respite from bustling Haverhill.**

House (Greek Revival and Italian Villa), the 1853 Goodell House, and the 1844 Kingsbury Home (part Greek Revival).

This abundance of historic architecture helped land Bradford on the National Register of Historic Places in 1977. Also listed is the Bradford Burial Ground, on Salem Street very close to the town green. The one-acre cemetery, established in 1655, has a marker with a date of 1689, although it is believed by local historians that even older burials exist.

The town green sits right there as a prominent piece of that village charm, with is shaded oasis that includes benches, paved walkways, dedication monuments, and a bandstand. The Bradford First Church of Christ faces the town green to lend a wonderfully familiar traditional New England look. Summer concerts on the common serve as the main attraction, but Bradford College and church family reunions also take place here, according to the Haverhill Historical Society.

Haverhill has deep industrial roots and is densely populated with nearly nineteen hundred people per square mile, so what a complete surprise to see a neighborhood like Bradford, with its big historic homes, a quaint village-like town green, and a more historic, refined appearance that looks more like Lexington and Concord than part of a bustling city. So, how did this neighborhood in Haverhill come to look significantly unlike any other section of Haverhill—one of the most famous shoe manufacturing cities in the United States from the 1830s to the early twentieth century?

Bradford was actually part of Rowley before coming together with Haverhill in 1897 (although in between, the east side of Bradford formed the town of Groveland in 1850), according to the Haverhill Historical Society. Even its association with Rowley was doomed from the beginning, as by 1670 enough families populated this neighborhood to form its own meetinghouse. Today this attractive Haverhill neighborhood—divided from the main parts of Haverhill by the Merrimack River—still has a feeling of being its own community with many residents preferring to say they are from Bradford rather than Haverhill, and has its own zip code and post office.

Churches have played a major role in Bradford history, with the east parish of Bradford located just off the Bradford town common. The church was established in 1726 and replaced by the current building in 1751. Academia in the Bradford Common Historic District has a longstanding tradition starting with the first school in 1701. By 1820, seven schoolhouses graced Bradford with, most prominently, the famous Bradford College founded in 1803 as first Bradford Academy and then Bradford Junior College before changing names again in 1971, according to the Haverhill Historical Society. Sadly, Bradford College fell into significant financial debt and closed in 2000. Fortunately, the campus was purchased for Northpoint Bible College in 2008—an institution known for its theology programs.

# CBRIDGEWATER

When thinking of college towns in Massachusetts, Cambridge and Amherst come to mind, but Bridgewater should also be placed on the "dean's list" when it comes to bustling communities with an academic vibe. With a leafy downtown featuring numerous mom-and-pop shops, historic homes, churches, and municipal buildings, the main attraction that elevates this southeastern Massachusetts downtown to something special is the town green. The circular common—residing in the middle of Main Street—provides a pleasing oasis with a dense front-to-end row of trees, comfortable benches, paved walkways, numerous dedication sites, expert landscaping, and brilliantly colored flower beds (most prominent) in the spring. Seasonal events like Christmas on the Common bring people together on the common, although daily use of the town green is significantly more than the average Massachusetts town common—perhaps because of the college crowd and a high number of senior citizens and families in town.

A one-of-a-kind plaque sits on the Bridgewater town green— dedicated to Mickey Cochrane, a native of Bridgewater and one of the greatest catchers of all time as a member of legendary manager Connie Mack's Philadelphia A's, as well as the Detroit Tigers during the 1920s and 1930s. The plaque reads, MAY HIS LEADERSHIP AND FIERCE COMPETITIVE SPIRIT BE AN INSPIRATION TO THE YOUTH OF BRIDGEWATER.

Although the town green's look suggests a deep-rooted history, research reveals that the common didn't really start forming until the 1820s—old indeed, but not so old when compared to the oldest Massachusetts town greens.

**Patriotic pride surrounds the Bridgewater town green.**

Bridgewater experienced a rather interesting beginning in 1656 that proves that Massachusetts towns that start one way don't necessarily evolve in that fashion. Local historian Bob Wood says that Bridgewater was part of West Bridgewater (a smaller town today than Bridgewater). With Plymouth not too far away, Pilgrims discovered this region as ideal for agriculture, as Plymouth was not a great candidate for farming with its rocky topography. The Pilgrims traveled more than three thousand miles to settle in Plymouth—what was another fourteen miles to Bridgewater in search of an ideal agriculture setting?

Most of the 1800s and 1900s saw Bridgewater evolve into an industrial town, however, famous for its iron works factories (a few still in business today), as well as paper mills, saw mills, and a boot and shoe factory, according to Wood. The boot and shoe factory no longer operates, but the building remains, along with many businesses and storage units, in close proximity to the town green. These industries helped the town common grow, with its village-like appeal eventually offering restaurants and shopping for the working class and their bosses. Neighborhoods near the town green reveal some spectacular Colonial and Victorian homes, with other dwellings appearing modest—thus suggesting various levels of available housing depending upon class.

Today Bridgewater is best known as the home of Bridgewater State University, a thriving public liberal arts university located right off the common. Bridgewater State was founded in 1840. While that qualifies as a historic presence, the oldest educational building belongs to the Bridgewater Academy Building, established in 1799 for "the purpose of promoting piety, religion and morality, and for the education of youth in such languages and in search of the liberal arts, as the Trustees hereinafter shall direct." The 1799 structure gave way to a new building in 1822 located at the south side of the town green on land donated by Major John Lazell (an iron works creator). Currently part of the Bridgewater Town Hall complex (very close to the town green) but once located right off the common, the school suspended operations in 1875 "due to the lack of sufficient patronage," according to the Plymouth County Registry of Deeds Notable Land Records Collection. The Town of Bridgewater owns the property, which was used as Bridgewater High School until 1952. Although now part of the Town Hall complex, the building stands proud and tall as a signature historical structure near the town green and serves as a "reminder of the role that small private academies played in education throughout Massachusetts during that era," states the Plymouth County Registry of Deeds Notable Land Records Collection.

While education has played a major role in Bridgewater's development, there's also an old-school element that reveals a hometown pride element. My Sister and I restaurant, as an example, has been around since the early 1980s and overlooks the town common. Conversations flow as much as the coffee, and locals prefer to take the two front seats overlooking the town green. With an old pay phone, orders sometimes written down on guest checks, and no credit cards accepted, My Sister and I seems as old-fashioned as the town common, even if modern celebrities like Steven Tyler of Aerosmith and former New England Patriots quarterback Drew Bledsoe have eaten here.

"It's a nice place to be," says Barbara Cyr of the Bridgewater town common. As the sister of My Sister and I owner Robert Ginn, Cyr adds, "A friend takes my son, Jacob, out there to play, and he has a great time."

Cyr and Ginn add that they especially like the lights and Santa's arrival on the common during the Christmas season, the Easter bunny visiting during the Easter season, and occasional church weddings.

# BROOKFIELD

If Hollywood chose to make a movie centered around a small New England town with an attractive town common, Brookfield could quite possibly be the main attraction. It's not a glamorous town, mind you, but rather a "real" place with that classic small town USA look. Like many New England towns, the designated historic district—also added to the National Register of Historic Places in 1990—is the best place to get a sense of what Brookfield is all about. Quiet, scenic, and seemingly a town of the past that made it to the twenty-first century in its retro form, the Brookfield town green comprises much of the Brookfield Common Historic District that extends from Route 148 to Main Street. Where most small, rural Massachusetts towns feature old homes that are spaced out around a town common, the Brookfield Historic District modestly showcases a slightly more dense concentration of more than one hundred older homes and buildings in the Federal, Greek Revival, and ltalianette styles, including the Brookfield Town Hall (Colonial Revival Style, 1904), Merrick Public Library (Queen Anne Style, 1883), and the Congregational Church (Romanesque Revival, 1857)—the latter two gracefully overlooking the town common. Some of the buildings were constructed for workers at shoe factories in the second half of the nineteenth century (the industry has sadly left Brookfield, though).

Structures surrounding the common are located close to the sidewalk, thus allowing locals and visitors a better chance to experience the town "up front"—that is, it's almost like walking through an outdoor museum depicting the heart of small town New England with its town common, homes, and buildings on display just steps away. The

31

A Brookfield town common memorial with bronze tablets recognizing the contribution of local men in the Civil War, the Spanish-Mexican War, and World War II.

whole scene might look merely "pleasant" when driving through, but it's highly recommended to get out of the car and walk this wonderfully old-fashioned, unspoiled area.

That town green, also known as Banister Common, proves that today's world can turn out something better than in the older days. The town green first started out as an eight-acre grassy slope, but in 1735 a local named Joseph Banister sold the land for the town to use as a militia field. That militia field eventually shrank to its current 1.3 acres in the form of a parklike setting for locals to enjoy.

The town green is about as nice as its gets in New England, with the right combination of shade, former cow paths now meant for human strolling, and a gazebo with a smattering of welcoming benches surrounding the structure. The "parts" of the town green might not be any different from other commons in Massachusetts, but somehow the sum feels more substantial and meaningful. Perhaps this is due, in part, to its overall consistency. No area of the town green looks uncared for, and it seems like each and virtually every home and building surrounding the common is filled with history and a lovingly maintained, well-preserved appearance. It feels safe, friendly (the people here are so nice!), and like the perfect hometown. Add its cozy hilltop location just north of the scenic Quaboag River (ideal for kayaking and canoeing) and its apple farm orchards surroundings, and you have the idyllic little town that, contrary to  societal public perception, seemed to disappear many years ago. This is not the case, though, in Brookfield. Currier and Ives and Norman Rockwell would have loved this district, as modern-day obstructions have found homes elsewhere.

There's also a fabulous monument located in the triangle section of the common, separated by a road from the main town green: a memorial with bronze tablets recognizing the contribution of local men in the Civil War, Spanish-Mexican War,  and World War II.

The Apple Country Fair is Brookfield's pride and joy event, and is appropriately located on the town green as the central gathering place. The Brookfield Community Club has organized this event since 1979 with highlights including local crafters, live music, children's games, baked goods, raffles, and a beloved tradition—an apple pie contest. A quilt is the centerpiece of the Apple Country Fair, as it takes nearly a year to make and is showcased in the center of the town common. It is also the first prize in a raffle! Typically held on the second Saturday of October, the Apple Country Fair also gives back to the community. Here is an excerpt from the Apple Country Fair website (http://applecountryfair.com) about the giving nature of this event: "The Brookfield Community Club has helped pay transportation costs for the Brookfield Elementary School's sixth grade class to attend a environmental program at Camp Bournedale on Cape Cod and generated grant money for a number of community service projects, from the town's monthly newsletter, the *Brookfield Citizen*, to holiday programs for Brookfield seniors."

Some other popular town common events include the Brookfield Tree Lighting Ceremony with Santa and a holiday house-decorating contest, which is usually held the first Sunday of December. Concerts on the common have been held on Friday during the summer. Memorial Day and Veterans Day observances take place annually. Also, the annual Brookfield Father's Day BBQ is held at the Brookfield Fire Department right near the green.

# BURLINGTON

Burlington is home to one of the biggest collective shopping centers in the northeastern United States, with the Burlington Mall, Wayside Commons, the Middlesex Commons Shopping Center, and Burlington Crossroads. The Lahey Clinic has also grown from nothing more than a small community hospital to one of the most comprehensive, largest hospitals in New England, and one with a global reputation—noteworthy, given the Boston area's reputation as home to some of the best hospitals in the world. It's hard to believe with the modern look of Burlington that this town was settled in 1641 and incorporated in 1799.

Most of the town's earlier days, however, centered on its presence as a major agricultural center with hops and rye production and the sales of fruits, vegetables, and milk to nearby Boston markets. All that changed from the mid-1950s to mid-1960s, when the state built Route 128 as a commuter highway. Soon Burlington became the fastest-growing town in the state and even tripled its population, thanks to commercial and residential development. There's very little room left to build in its relatively small 11.9 square miles with a population of around twenty-four thousand. Astonishingly, in addition to those twenty-four thousand residents, approximately one hundred thousand people work in this town every weekday.

Today, much of Burlington is surely fast-paced; it's often congested with traffic and with just about every convenience a suburbanite could ever want. Add several mini shopping centers, hotels, and a terrific variety of restaurants, and the town feels completely different from when, as late as the mid-1960s, cows could be seen grazing the

**Burlington Veterans Memorial Park at the town green.**

field at the current Burlington Mall location. That was Burlington then—a sleepy town with a low population and a much slower pace.

That town remarkably still remains, although visitors know nothing about the "old town," as it is tucked away from all the commercial conveniences. Driving a few miles north on Route 1A off Route 128 reveals the best representation of retro Burlington—the town common, of course. The space is huge, certainly one the largest in suburban Boston. Paved paths meander parts of the town green, but much of the space requires walking the grass. Like many Massachusetts town greens, the Burlington town common has a bandstand, benches, and many historical buildings surrounding the property.

Controversy circled around having a bandstand back in the early 1970s, with town meeting discussions about whether the bandstand would attract hedonistic rock bands and "people of the so-called drug culture," according to the History Stands Still: The Background of Bandstands Throughout New England website (http://bandstands .blogspot.com). Those opposed opined that the "hippies would trample their lush common area and vandals would have a field day with the bandstand."

Without a thought that the former Musicland record store at the Burlington Mall brought in, and employed, the counterculture in droves and the fact that many garage band were making significant noise in myriad Burlington neighborhoods during that generation, the culture was already implanted in this then very conservative town. Common sense prevailed, though, and in July 1973, Joseph Visco, an employee of the Burlington Recreation Department, along with other staff members designed and constructed the bandstand. The Murray family, of Burlington, contributed more than four thousand dollars to the project in honor of their father, Theodore G. Murray, who helped grow the commercial and residential element of Burlington. The bandstand was dedicated to his memory in ceremonies on August 11, according to History Stands Still: The Background of Bandstands Throughout New England. The bandstand looks like a traditional New England gazebo and fits in beautifully in the center of the sprawling Burlington town green.

The greatest drawing card at the Burlington town common, however, is the Burlington Veterans Memorial Park, as this ambitiously designed dedication area truly stands out as a great reminder of those who have served. Monuments include a grand memorial to those who gave their lives to protect our freedoms, a separate stone for Marines who have served, a tribute from the Burlington Lions Club to John F. Kennedy, a huge American flag and smaller ones dotting the landscape, five thirty-foot-tall flags representing each branch of the military, and a replica of an 1838 cannon. Adding further utmost respect to our military is the area's meticulous and thoughtful landscaping that includes lighting and benches. It is simply one of the best town green military dedication sites in all of Massachusetts and is ideal for Veterans and Memorial Day observances, as well as post-9/11 ceremonies.

"It's a very nice feeling," says Bob Hogan, the recently retired veterans agent for the Town of Burlington and an Army veteran who served in Vietnam from 1967 to 1968. "When you drive up the hill from the old Building 19, you see the flags on the right. The town didn't pay for it (with the exception of landscaping), locals supported it."

Those involved with the project added flagpoles and walls in 2013, and a few years before that, consolidated all the dedication monuments and markers into the current Memorial Park.

"They took down a lot of bushes, so it doesn't feel restrictive," says Hogan. "Looking down the hill, you can see the whole town common, so everything comes together very well. When there's just enough of a breeze on a sunny day and you see that red, white, and blue flag, it's quite a feeling."

Simonds Park, across the street, was originally regarded as part of the town green, but is now considered separate, as it is overseen by the Town Recreation Department, while the town common is managed by the Board of Selectmen. Simonds Park, however, provides a wonderful family experience with one of the most impressive playgrounds in all of suburban Boston with its age-appropriate sections of play areas, lighted tennis courts, a great baseball field, and an outdoor swimming area.

Burlington has always gotten great use out of its town common. Growing up my first six years in Burlington, I remember the Burlington Recreation and Parks Department's summer activities and then seeing that tradition continue in my twenties when I became the assistant editor of the now-defunct *Burlington News* weekly newspaper. Donald Roberts held the position of Recreation Director for thirty-seven years until his retirement in 2009. He grew the department from twenty to two hundred programs, many showcasing wonderful community gathering scenes of American life—especially for the kids—on the town green for the world to see. It was pure magic, and the robust recreation department offerings, fortunately, continue to this very day. It's quite a contrast to the densely populated retail and restaurant scene just a few minutes away.

Public events include Concerts on the Common on Tuesday and movie nights on Wednesday during the summer; Celebrate Burlington, a town day, of sorts, typically held the first Saturday of August; frequent weddings at the gazebo; the tree lighting ceremony on the first Sunday of December (with fireworks); Truck Day (new, antique, all types!) on the Sunday of Labor Day weekend; and Memorial Day, Veterans Day, and 9/11 observances.

# CAMBRIDGE

Cambridge Common Park—also known as the Harvard Square Common—has an ideal location adjacent to Harvard University and bustling Harvard Square with all its interesting shops and restaurants. A National Historic Landmark dating back to 1630 (when Cambridge was known as Newtowne), this sixteen-acre town green gets put to great use with nearly ten thousand pedestrians and cyclists using the paths and sidewalks daily, according to the City of Cambridge website.

Providing a much-needed spot for locals, students, and tourists visiting the urban environs of Cambridge, the town green isn't just about walkways and benches. The 2009 renovated Arthur W. Kemp playground, states the City of Cambridge website, features "a landscape of hills, valleys, sand, wooden branches and stumps, living plant material, and loose wooden blocks to build with. It is a place where kids can invent their own forms of play. Many features are made from naturally decay-resistant wood. Slides are embedded into hills. Turning a crank sends water cascading down a series of tables into the sand area. There is a swing set for toddlers, a multidirectional dish-shaped swing that can be used by several children at once, a seesaw with multiple seats at each end for groups of children (or adults), and a 'merry-go-round' that is at ground level to provide wheelchair access."

Cliff Gallant, who has lived in Cambridge most of his life, appreciates the family opportunities at the Cambridge Common. "I have fond memories of the park," says Gallant. "I used to go there with my sons Owen and Conal—they had this giant netting here you could climb to the top of the hill. We used to play hide and seek, and I

**Cambridge City Common serves as an oasis in the middle of the city.** BILL DEIGNAN, CAMBRIDGE COMMUNITY DEVELOPMENT DEPARTMENT

always thought it was so cool. It's the type of place where parents are really interactive with their kids, not just a place where kids are on their own."

Bounded by Massachusetts Avenue, Garden Street, and Waterhouse Street, the Cambridge Common has actually shrunk significantly through its long-time existence. The beginnings featured essential needs for that period of time by serving as a gathering place for military training, town meetings, social events, and burial ground, according to the Cambridge Historical Society. The city also put aside a parcel known as the Cow Common as a source for fuel and food. But that changed as Cambridge became more urbanized during the early to mid-1800s.

The stories at the Cambridge Common are legendary. Thousands of soldiers camped here for several months in 1775 where General George Washington drew his sword and led the way, formally taking command of the Continental Army. William Dawes rode through the Common on Paul Revere's famous midnight ride. The Cambridge

Historical Tours website states, "Though credited for being Paul Revere's 'sidekick' in most popular lore, Dawes rode 17 miles before falling off his horse. Revere only rode 13 before his arrest."

Several memorials pay honor to the history here, including a commemorative plaque marking the location of the Washington Elm—a tree where Washington allegedly stood when assuming command of the Continental Army; a Civil War memorial with a statue of Abraham Lincoln and a soldier; the Irish Famine Memorial, dedicated on July 23, 1997, by then-president of Ireland, Mary Robinson; three bronze cannons; a plaque for Henry Knox; and a memorial for Tadeusz Kościuszko, a Polish military leader who also fought in the American Revolutionary War as a colonel in the Continental Army.

# COHASSET

There's this fallacy that towns by the ocean don't have nice town greens. Let's just say that theory is out to sea.

The beautiful coastal South Shore town of Cohasset certainly refutes the landlocked town green theory by offering a long rectilinear town common that is among the most picturesque in Massachusetts. The expansive town green is surrounded by twenty-seven remarkable-looking homes that are predominantly Georgian and Federal-style architecture (with later styles including Colonial, Gothic, Greek, Queen Anne, and Second Empire), three churches, the First Parish Meeting House of 1747, a rectory, and Cohasset Town Hall. Interestingly, local housewrights (basically, a craftsman who cut timber, like a lumberjack, in the quantity required for the construction of a house) built many of the homes in the historic district rather than experienced architects.

Cohasset was conceived as common land at the earliest division of lands in 1670—and became a town separate from Hingham in 1770.

The town green features a scenic small pond and plenty of benches to enjoy pond views and broad, open landscape steeped in classic, traditional New England looks. The town green features several memorials, mostly honoring military citizens.

All this and plenty of historic elements landed the twenty-four-acre Cohasset Common Historic District on the National Register of Historic Places in 1996. The historic neighborhood has also been recognized by Massachusetts as an official historic district—so the overlay of local, state, and national historic designation protects the integrity of Cohasset's wonderful preservation. But, before all the appropriate

The Cohasset town green features a beautiful pond and is surrounded by historic structures.

designations, Cohasset sought that preservation many years ago: Townsfolk in 1937 instituted a visionary incentive to protect the historic village center, whose earliest house dates to 1713, according to the Trust for Architectural Easements website (http://architecturaltrust .org/easements/about-the-trust/trust-protected-communities/historic -districts-in-massachusetts/cohasset-common-historic-district/). That excellent decision has resulted in a Massachusetts town that has few rivals when it comes to historical integrity.

"I walk on a rise from Beach Street to meet the Common," says Kathyrn Wells, a Cohasset resident. "Having just climbed from a spectacular, windy, open view of Little Harbor, I find that the embrace of the historic homes, churches, and town offices around the common's plateau provides a mindful, centering, grounding feeling. Here I rest on the bench at the base of the enormous flagpole and gaze out across the autumn grass to the tower of the historic Unitarian meetinghouse. A stark white, quintessentially New England portrait settles in against a gray sky. Here, I am surely at peace."

Most popular events on the town green include the South Shore Arts Festival on Father's Day weekend, the tree lighting at the Common with Santa in December, and the farmers' market on Thursday in the summer.

The Cohasset town green also can boast a few Hollywood moments. *The Witches of Eastwick* (1987), starring Jack Nicholson, Susan Sarandon, Cher, and Michelle Pfeiffer, featured a scene at the common. *Housesitter* (1992), starring Goldie Hawn, also featured Cohasset town green scenes, as well as scenes at the village center and neighborhoods.

Just a few steps away from the quaint village center with many fine shops and restaurants—and a mile from the ocean—the Cohasset town green can serve as a standalone destination or part of a fun day in one of the state's most underrated coastal towns.

# CONCORD

Concord needs no introduction with its Revolutionary War roots. Given its rich history, it's no surprise that Concord has a splendid village green: Monument Square.

Located in the center of town within the Concord Monument Square–Lexington Road Historic District, Monument Square is saturated with history. The historic district, established in 1635, became one of the first English settlements away from the coast.

As a precursor to the birthplace of our nation, soldiers occupied Concord, marching through what is now known as Monument Square. On April 19, 1775, the first day of the war, Bullet Hole House situated north of the Monument Square at North Bridge, became a symbol of the Revolutionary War. The house still has a hole from the bullet fired during the North Bridge battle.

Ralph Waldo Emerson, in his 1836 poem "Concord Hymn," described the Bullet Hole House in legendary terms as the location of "the shot heard 'round the world."

He said of the town green, "Crossing a bare common, in snow puddles, at twilight, under a clouded sky, without having in my thoughts any occurrence of special good fortune, I have enjoyed a perfect exhilaration. I am glad to the brink of fear."

Concord's Monument Square also serves as an excellent foundation for touring several sites that center around famous American essayist, poet, and philosopher Henry David Thoreau.

Thoreau, often erroneously labeled as a loner and cranky misanthrope, actually exhibited deep involvement with townsfolk in an effort to make Concord a better community—even if he was publicly

**The thirty-foot-tall granite Civil War obelisk stands proudly at Concord's Monument Square.**

critical of them. Call him the early day version of the notorious town meeting member at modern-day town meetings in New England, often throwing verbal bombs at people and policies perceived as detrimental to the town.

Before becoming the famous "Hermit of Walden Pond," many of his experiences centered around the Monument Square area. From 1835 to 1837 he actually lived at what is now known as Concord's Colonial Inn (a lodging and restaurant destination) right off Monument Square while attending Harvard College in Cambridge, Massachusetts—thus making him one of the most famous commuting students in the history of the United States! After graduating

Harvard, Thoreau served as a schoolhouse teacher at the northwest side of Monument Square, but he left because of the school's policy on corporal punishment, according to the National Park Service (NPS) website page on Concord's Monument Square (www.nps.gov/ nr/travel/massachusetts_conservation/concord_monument_square .html). The NPS website adds that Thoreau even spent time in jail on the west side of Monument Square because of tax evasion with a current-day marker noting his arrest and famous subsequent essay, "Civil Disobedience." Thoreau, clearly a keen observer of life, could see the town common reflected society's changes:

> When I came out of prison . . . I did not perceive that great changes had taken place on the common, such as he observed who went in a youth and emerged a tottering and gray-headed man; and yet a change had to my eyes come over the scene—the town, and State, and country—greater than any that mere time could effect.

Like Emerson, "Thoreau first practiced his written essays as speeches before local audiences at the Concord Lyceum in a free lecture series sponsored by the town," according to NPS. The NPS goes on to report that many of Thoreau's lectures—that took on the form of passionate speeches—occurred in public buildings at Monument Square, including the Masonic Hall and the Town House. Thoreau presented nineteen talks at the Concord Lyceum between 1838 to 1860, covering a wide range of topics including "Concord River" (1845); "White Beans and Walden Pond" (1849); "The Wild, or Walking" (1851); "Autumn Tints" (1859); and "Wild Apples" (1860). He also presented a speech on forest succession to the Middlesex Agricultural Society on September 20, 1860, in the Town House.

During the nineteenth century locals constructed many buildings at or near Monument Square that give Concord its wonderfully familiar historic look today. That includes the Concord Town House built for government use in 1851 and the homes of the Emersons, Alcotts, and Hawthornes. The early twentieth century saw the Concord Art

Association form, which moved into the John Ball House, according to the NPS website.

With all this historical activity through the years, it is no surprise that Concord Monument Square was listed in the National Register of Historic Places in 1977. Today the most prominent monuments and markers at Monument Square are a thirty-foot-tall granite Civil War obelisk; a plaque honoring twenty-five residents that died in World War I (the plaque also includes poetry verses written by Emerson); a plaque attached to a boulder honoring three residents killed in the Spanish–American War; and a small plaza with three memorials honoring those who lost their lives in World War II, Korea, Vietnam, Iraq, and the US occupation of the Dominican Republic in 1965 to 1966.

Even though Concord had an agricultural presence before and during its incorporation, Monument Square does not represent that rural past in regard to appearance.

"Monument Square doesn't have the same feeling as other New England town commons," says Leslie Perrin Wilson, a curator with the Concord Free Public Library. "Most of them were about open space and cattle grazing. Monument Square has more structure over a pastoral feeling."

Monument Square is, to no surprise, one of the locations for the Patriots Day Parade—featuring Revolutionary War reenactments, as well as parades and other relevant events—held annually on the third Monday of April (otherwise known as Patriots Day Weekend in Massachusetts).

A great place to learn about Monument Square is at the Concord Museum (200 Lexington Road; 508-369-9753; www.concordmuseum.org), about a ten-minute walk from Monument Square. This landmark Concord attraction offers a wealth of artifacts and general information on Concord's history. The Concord Free Library at 129 Main Street also offers a great selection of publications on Concord history—the building is about a seven-minute walk to Monument Square.

# DANA

Dana doesn't exist anymore. When the Commonwealth of Massachusetts built the Quabbin Reservoir in the 1930s as the state's main drinking water–supply source, places like Dana were virtually dismantled to accommodate the massive, important project. Virtually all that can be seen today in this once-vibrant community is a well-defined town green with some leftover elements in the area: extant foundations and cellar holes, granite steps, fragments of paving, stone fence posts, walls, and a metal safe too big and heavy to relocate, according to the National Park Service (NPS) website (www.nps.gov/nr/travel/massachusetts_conservation/dana_common.html).

Once part of neighboring Petersham and Hardwick, Dana became its own town in 1801 and once featured, states NPS, a "town store and post office, the former Baptist meetinghouse purchased and relocated from Petersham to become Dana's town hall and first school room, and the hotel and tavern [that] all brought commercial activity to the village." Summer visitors flocked to Dana and other Swift River area towns, enjoying the picturesque, relaxing rural surroundings.

Now virtually nothing is left but the triangular-shaped town common, which can be accessed 1.7 miles down the road from Gate 40, off Route 32A in Petersham. Access is by foot or bicycle. The Quabbin Visitor Center, located at 485 Ware Road (Route 9) in Belchertown, offers more information on Dana and is open daily from 9:00 a.m. to 4:30 p.m., except on major holidays. Because Dana is located within the Quabbin drinking water–supply area and managed by Department of Conservation and Recreation, there are certain rules for visiting the area (like no dogs allowed). For more information on rules and regulations,

**Dana is a village that doesn't exist anymore due to the construction of the Quabbin Reservoir in the 1930s.** CLIF READ/MA DEPARTMENT OF CONSERVATION AND RECREATION, QUABBIN RESERVOIR

log onto www.mass.gov/eea/agencies/dcr/water-res-protection/water shed-mgmt/general-rules-and-regulations-concerns-public-use-access .html.

According to Clif Read, supervisor of interpretative services at the Department of Conservation and Recreation, Quabbin Section, in Ware, there are no annual town green events to report in Dana, although school presentations and an annual Dana Reunion take place in the lost village. Amazingly, as of this writing, approximately sixty former residents who lived in Dana or any of the Swift River towns attend the reunion!

# DEDHAM

Drive through areas of Dedham and you'll see Boston-like neighborhoods with densely populated residential streets, a significant commercial base—especially the 675,000 square foot Legacy Place open-air retail environment—and myriad industrial areas. Arrive in "Precinct One," however, and the whole landscape changes with the Dedham Village Historic District.

Geographically located near the center of town and bordering Boston (West Roxbury and Hyde Park), the nearly fifty-five acres of this magnificent district include "234 buildings, six sites, and seven objects [that] contribute to its architectural and historical integrity," according to information presented on the "National Register of Historic Places (NRHP) Dedham Village Historic District" application form from July 2006. That's no surprise, however, given that Dedham—settled in 1635 by people from Roxbury and Watertown and officially incorporated in 1636—is one of the oldest communities in the state.

The Great Common, also known as the Training Ground, shows its traditional New England beauty within a triangular shape bounded by High, Common, and Dexter Streets and is surrounded by stately nineteenth- and early twentieth-century residential development. Bisected by Bridge Street (since 1828), The Common is much smaller than it once was, but residents continue to frequent this green space, thus following past generations that have done exactly the same since 1644. There's also a "Little Common"—a rectangular area at the front of the First Parish Church at High and Court Streets. This small area is the last open space from the original 1638 landholdings of the First Church. As an interesting side note, the first tax-supported, free, and

**The Dedham town green is triangular shaped and unspoiled.**

public school in the United States was "built in 1644 and stood near the Church while the town's first public library was in the minister's office (then later the church vestry) from 1795 to 1855," states the First Church and Parish Dedham website's "375 Years of History in Short" article (www.dedhamuu.org).

Today historic detached residential dwellings range from the mid-eighteenth century to the first quarter of the twentieth century, with Federal and Greek Revival styles dominating, although many Georgian and Colonial Revival remain. Additionally, "four churches, four Norfolk County government buildings (two courthouses, a registry of deeds and a former correctional facility), the historical society and a library exhibit a wide range of styles including 19th-century Greek Revival to 20th-century Art Deco in design, although the majority date from the 19th-century and are architect-designed examples," according to the NRHP application form.

Placed on the NRHP in 2006—and with the Norfolk County Courthouse as a National Landmark—Dedham has held onto its glorious past with truly fabulous historic preservation. Additionally, the modern-day downtown, with its impressive mix of shops, restaurants, and a renovated old-time movie theater, stands as one of the most attractive, nicely utilized central districts in small- to medium-size towns within metro Boston.

# DEERFIELD

Nothing says "New England" quite like the "Old Deerfield" historic village neighborhood of Deerfield. With two dozen eighteenth-century and at least a dozen nineteenth-century buildings lining its nearly mile-long quaint, tree-lined Main Street, this trip-back-in-time town off the main road offers one of the most unspoiled, authentic Colonial America scenes in New England. Settled in 1669, Deerfield is a rarity, one of the only towns formed by English colonists along the Eastern seaboard that preserves its "original scale and town plan," according to the Historic Deerfield website (www.historic-deerfield .org/discover-deerfield/village-overview/). It's quite a contrast to the most popular modern-day Deerfield-area attractions like the Yankee Candle Factory with its ninety-thousand-square-foot facility located in South Deerfield!

For tourists who love historic towns, Deerfield offers guided and self-guided tours of twelve period museum houses dating from circa 1730 to 1872, the Flynt Center of Early New England Life, and the Memorial Libraries that all serve as great starting points. So rich is the history that "Old Deerfield" founded Historic Deerfield Inc., a formally created outdoor history museum that "focuses on the history and culture of the Connecticut River Valley and early New England." But it's not just about old homes and buildings in Old Deerfield—that is, Historic Deerfield is committed to preserving, states the Historic Deerfield website, "collections of regional furniture, silver, textiles, and other decorative arts."

Adding nationally known additional layers of traditional New England are the Deerfield Inn, a classic New England inn from 1884

The Deerfield town common is well cared for within this famous historic New England village.

that is a National Historic Landmark offering lodging as well as dining from its restaurant and tavern; Deerfield Academy, a boarding school founded in 1797; and the Bement School, a center of education for kindergarten to ninth grade that dates back to 1925.

The search for Colonial America in our modern-day world certainly doesn't get much better than visiting Old Deerfield Village, but what would a historic community like this be without a town green? Happily, in this great little town located within what is known as the Happy Valley, a town green does exist and it's an underrated beauty.

Visitors to Deerfield often bypass the town green in lieu of a route that leads to all the historical attractions, but what they don't realize is that this open space offers equally historic significance and ambiance. A book entitled *Historical Collections, being a General Collection of Interesting Facts, Traditions, Biographical Sketches, Anecdotes,* published in 1839, states that a local named William Barber made a woodcut of forested land into a town green in 1838 to accommodate the open space in a New England town center that served as a park to stroll, a space for militia training days in the fall and spring, and a location for an a old brick schoolhouse that was replaced for a new brick schoolhouse—now known as the First Church of Deerfield—to be used as a meetinghouse for religious worship.

The most striking scene on the Deerfield town green is the recently restored and restructured thirty-eight-foot-high brownstone Civil War monument, which could possibly be one of the first Civil War monuments erected in the state, according to several locals.

Today the town green is not as extensive as before, but like surrounding historic structures, fits in perfectly as part of Deerfield's outdoor living museum concept. Surrounded by Deerfield Academy, old homes, and the aforementioned First Church of Deerfield, the town common feels like a mini oasis set within a bigger oasis—that is, one of the last remaining "pure" New England colonial villages remaining in the six-state region.

From the south side of the common, the juxtaposition of an American flag, the monument, and the church—complemented by the shaded parklike grounds—makes for a scene that could quite well serve this genre as the prototype for a classic Massachusetts town green. There's an added "X-factor" to walking the town green, too, that can't be fully described but might have something to do with the sweet smell of plant life, the fresh country air, and the myriad trees converging to create a sort of secure, safe haven from the rest of the world. Although many people walk through the town common, few stop to experience this wonderful feeling that, in other towns, might be impeded by noisy transportation and other modern-day societal sounds that were obviously nonexistent in Colonial times. The absence of suburban and urban sounds at the town green and virtually all of Historic Deerfield lends further purity to what almost, sadly, seems like an anomaly in New England, where commercial, residential, industrial, and recreational growth encroaches upon the historic template of Massachusetts.

The town green does not host most of Deerfield's major seasonal events; rather the nearby Memorial Hall Museum takes the lead with events like the Fall Craft Fair, July 4th festivities, and summer concerts.

For more on the town green or to take tours of Old Deerfield, visit the Visitor Center at Hall Tavern, or contact (413) 775-7132 or tours@historic-deerfield.org.

# DORCHESTER (BOSTON)

Hundreds of thousands tourists visit Boston every year; the city's incredible history and preservation are major drawing cards. They visit the Freedom Trail, Faneuil Hall, the Boston Common, and historical churches and museums, but the interesting part is that visitors often completely miss out on Boston's first settlement, as it isn't located in any tourist area.

Reverend Allen Park, originally Dorchester Common during the area's first settlement in 1630, stands as one of the most historically significant areas of Massachusetts. Located on Meetinghouse Hill (that should give you a clue!), the park features a monument to soldiers who fought in the Civil War. While clearly an important monument, that doesn't even begin to tell the history of this neighborhood. You have to look around the area to find the historic jewels. One is the First Parish Church—initially built in the early 1700s as a crude log cabin thatched with grass before the sixth and final building was constructed in 1897.

Puritans founded the church, as well as the first elementary school supported by public money in the New World—the Cotton Mather School located behind the First Parish. Puritans held the first town meeting at the church, which determined policy through open and frequent discussions.

**A Civil War monument and the First Parish Church lend a historic feel to this Dorchester hilltop neighborhood.**

The First Parish of Dorchester website elaborates on the area's fascinating history:

The first four meetinghouses acted as Dorchester's town hall. The fifth building, built in 1816, was the host to many social justice leaders, such as William Lloyd Garrison and Theodore

Parker, because of First Parish's long-standing pastor Reverend Nathaniel Hall who was dedicated to the abolitionist cause. In the 1880s, the work of First Parish's minister, Christopher R. Eliot, and the Fields Corner Congregational Church's minister, Reverend T.J. Volentine, inspired First Parish members and friends to organize the Fields Corner Industrial School for local children, which evolved into the Dorchester House, a multiservice health center. Church members continue to serve on its board of directors.

The Parish continues today to serve as a gathering place—but in more of a diverse way—for Vietnamese, African-American, Caribbean, Irish, Latino, Haitian, and Cape Verdean residents.

Near Reverend Allen Park other notable historical attractions reside. St. Peter's Church, built in 1872 from the puddingstone on which it rests, features stunning Neo-Gothic architecture. The eleven-plus-acre Ronan Park became a public park in 1912 when Boston acquired the land and is an Olmsted-designed site with amazing views of Boston Harbor and Dorchester Bay from the peak of Meetinghouse Hill. According to the City of Boston website, the annual Ronan Park Multicultural Festival takes place in August, with local food, bands, and performances.

# EAST BRIDGEWATER

Locals truly love their East Bridgewater town common, and why not? In this small, modest southeastern Massachusetts town not too far from Plymouth, the town green is the center of life in the most traditional New England ways. With two churches; old historic homes; the high school, middle school, and elementary schools; town hall; and police station virtually all within sight, this is how small Massachusetts towns used to be set up before succumbing to expansion. Despite the heavy rush hour traffic that reminds us we are indeed in the twenty-first century, take away that congestion and the town common area embodies a traditional New England small town layout at its best.

Margaret Alexander has lived near the town common her whole life, dating back to her birth in 1927. She married an East Bridgewater man, is part of a family that goes back ten generations in town, and would not live anywhere else. Her grandson lives across the street and her granddaughter is next door.

Alexander believes that the town common plays a major role in East Bridgewater's small town charm. She remembers as a child always looking forward to the Memorial Day observances. "East Bridgewater had these all-day celebrations at the town common," she says. "They had parades, band concerts and it always brought families together. We would also go across the street to see the soldiers' gravestones in

**The expansive East Bridgewater town green resides in the middle of a well-preserved historic district.**

the cemetery. I liked to see the vets in uniform, it left me in awe. It was always a great day. East Bridgewater is such a patriotic town."

Alexander says that other town and church activities at or near the town common made this district special, including church movies and plays, winter events, and several weddings a year. The post-Vietnam era brought a decline in town common use, says Alexander, but she has noticed a renewed interest over the past several years. She attributes part of that to East Bridgewater's population nearly tripling since the 1970s, with new families interested in community life. "They (the newer residents) see the beauty of the town," says Alexander.

Newer residents, that is, as young as Makena Hagan, who was born in 2012 and just moved with her parents, Sarah and Matt, to East Bridgewater. "I really like it here," says Makena, at just three years old. "It's fun to run on the red brick paths and across the grass. There are flags for the soldiers, too. I like coming here with my family."

Family, small town life, and special memories of the town common have made Margaret a believer in East Bridgewater. "I just love the town," says Alexander. "One time my husband had a pharmacy in Weymouth (about twenty minutes from East Bridgewater). We came to a point where, because of distance, we either had to sell the pharmacy and/or move. We sold the pharmacy."

Of the town green, she adds, "With the rectory and old homes, it looks much like it did in the 1930s."

The 1.7-mile triangular-shaped town common on its own—bounded by Central Street at its wide northern side, by Plymouth Street to its southwest, and Morse Avenue to its southeast—also represents the traditional New England town common quite well, with a nice gazebo and an attractive expanse of well-maintained green grass. A historically important center of activity as a public gathering place and militia training field (playing a role in the Revolutionary War) as well as a common pasturage in the very beginning, the town green today stands out with its fence of square granite posts and iron rails surrounding the town green and wooden park benches placed within the length of the space.

One of the more unusual events occurs in May, when there is a tribute to East Bridgewater's Civil War veterans. Approximately two dozen men wearing Union Army uniforms create the reenactment for hundreds of visitors. During prom time the gazebo is a popular place for photo opportunities. The town common also hosts Santa and a tree-lighting ceremony in December, occasional summer concerts, business fairs, and a town day. The town also hosts a Veterans Day ceremony every three years on the town common, as the town rotates the observance with neighboring Bridgewater and West Bridgewater, according to Alexander.

Dale Julius, who is part of the Civil War reenactment and has played town common concerts with his band, Dale and the Duds, for the past twenty-five-plus years, loves his town green. "It's the heartbeat of the town and beautiful to look at coming from a distance to arriving there," says Julius.

At the reenactment ceremonies, he and other participants would act as true-to-form as possible, holding musters and pitching tents to sleep at night on the town green. On the music side, Dale and the Duds have played to as many as fifteen hundred locals attending their town green concerts. "When the crowd goes home, I see the whole common empty and aesthetically pleasing and it's really a mystical thing," Julius says.

Julius has great early memories of town green carnivals, but he also remembers when the town green fell into disrepair with tall grass and deteriorating fencing. Controversy also circled the East Bridgewater town green when former Church of East Bridgewater minister Paul J. Rich envisioned a "Sturbridge/Williamsburg/Strawberry Bank concept," to his church with, according to the *Perkins v. Rich* legal case (http://masscases.com/cases/app/11/11massappct317.html), "work (that) included large scale construction obvious to all Church members such as: placement of a railroad car adjacent to the Church; interior renovation; extensive landscaping; two swimming pools, carpentry work . . . construction of parking lots."

This affected the town common, too, where Rich reportedly placed an art gallery and sculpture, as well as Vietnam anti-war postings. Financial setbacks, public opposition, and ultimately legal actions averted any further church use of the town green. In the late 1980s, East Bridgewater "rededicated" the town green, and the look and feel of the open space has been kept superbly.

As part of a sixty-nine-acre town historic district that was placed on the National Register of Historic Places in 1999, the East Bridgewater town green has many historic friends in the neighborhood. This includes, most prominently, the First Parish Church, whose "large scale and tall spire are visible from all parts of the district."

Nineteenth-century Federal, Colonial and Greek Revival homes—some with rear barns maintaining original design character—juxtapose with mature plantings and nicely landscaped grounds to create a well-established look for the historic district.

Situated on an elongated glacial formation historically known as "The Plain," this long level stretch runs the full length from west to east until a drop-off south of the town green and the southern boundary of the district. It's an unusual scene but yet so quintessentially New England!

Joan Kerrigan, who spent her first twenty years in East Bridgewater, has wonderful memories of the town common, and she feels grateful for the citizens' renewed interest in the green. She says:

Growing up in East Bridgewater was a blessing in so many ways, as it is a small town and everyone seemed to know each other, and look out for each other. It was warm and friendly and seemingly inviting. As a young girl, my family spent many summer evenings going to band concerts on the town common. People of all ages would take their folding aluminum with woven webbing lawn chairs and blankets and come out to the Common to catch a breeze and catch up with other families. My mother's cousin, Louis Forcier, played drums for a band combo that frequently played on the bandstand with Tony Ferrante on clarinet. Later, Tony's son, Robert, played drums in a 50s band called Dale and the Duds, with Dale Julius. I remember various organizations sold refreshments and there were kiddie games to play to keep youngsters occupied while parents and grandparents could sit to enjoy the fine summer evenings on the common. I also remember teenagers with their dates sitting on blankets, holding hands and enjoying the music. The common was a gathering place in town, and children used to run and play there.

Later, in the 70s, the common became an art gallery, of sorts, and seemingly taken over by the pastor of a local church. I remember a small model house/museum, which appeared to me as odd, was placed on the common and there was a general attitude that it was no longer a place to play. There was also a train car nearby, possibly as an artifact. At that time, the band concerts dwindled and the open, happy place seemed gloomy. Speculation and suspicion replaced the feel-good atmosphere and many parents no longer wanted their children to hang out in that area. Years later, the town reclaimed the area and restored the common grounds. Today, celebrations are held there, such as the Christmas tree decorating contest and Civil War re-enactments. Concerts are once again part of what the common has to offer the happy citizens of East Bridgewater.

# EASTHAM

Most visitors regard Eastham as a prime destination to access the Cape Cod National Seashore, a spectacular forty-mile stretch of expansive beaches and dunes along the Atlantic Ocean. With that in mind, it's, unfortunately, easy to bypass one of the most significantly historical areas of Cape Cod on Route 6 known as the Eastham Center National Register District. As Eastham is the oldest town among the several towns located on the "Lower Cape" (incorporated by a group of Pilgrims in 1651), the chance to see a fleeting element of Cape Cod—that is, a destination void of overdevelopment—is amazingly apparent within sight off a major road.

The town green was first developed in 1897 and today catches the eye for good reason: It is the only common in New England with a historic windmill. Suffice it to say, the town green is known as Windmill Park. Eastham resident Thomas Paine (not the Founding Fathers Thomas Paine!) constructed the octagonal-shaped windmill in 1680 in Plymouth and then moved it to Truro in 1770, followed by a temporary location in Eastham in 1793 before finding its permanent home in 1808, according to the Cape Cod neighborhoods Eastham Windmill web page (www.capecodneighborhoods.com/blog/the -historic-eastham-windmill.html).

The Eastham Windmill has become a beloved local attraction. Each year since 1977 the Eastham Windmill Festival takes place on the first weekend after Labor Day and features a sand art competition, road races, band concerts, an arts and crafts show, a tricycle race, a barbeque, and square dancing.

The Eastham town common features a windmill originally constructed in 1680.

"Two words: Windmill weekend!" says Sarah Duggan, of the festival weekend and her native town, in general. "The parade, local food, friends, family, and children. It's for everyone. No fast food or mini malls, just a small quiet town. Loved going there as a child. Grew up in this town till I was eighteen years old. Miss my little town where everyone knew everyone."

Chuck Glass, an Eastham native, says of Windmill Park, "It's what keeps a small town . . . small."

The local community has also lovingly cared for this one-of-a-kind Cape Cod structure and landmark. When repairs were needed to fix several areas of fencing around the windmill in 1996, a local Boy Scout Eagle Scout candidate started a project to raise funds to update the historic landmark. Local businesses provided all the funding, thus restoring the fence.

There's not much else to see within the grassy 1.6-acre town green except a split rail fence that encloses the area and a stone pump and watering trough standing east of the windmill. Despite going against every Massachusetts town green tenet—no monuments, markers, or gazebo—the town green retains that classic town common look and is quite popular as an inland oasis for locals. It's a perfect place for a stroll or to have a picnic.

"I love this common as for a few hours you can return to a time that is simple," says Eastham native Darlene Harrigan Brown. "It's a place where you can gather to meet neighbors, make friends and cherish old friends. Treasure the way life was, simple and caring. Love that my grandchildren can run free, feel free. It's an experience I can pass to them so they can learn to stop for a few hours and breathe. The windmill, for me, provides comfort, beauty, and the chance to relive a simpler time."

Local resident Tom Pope says, "The town green is a place of common ground where the threads of our diversity in music, culture, and the arts are woven together in commonality reflecting the strength of our values and traditions to form the fabric of a town we call Eastham."

Roger Dumas and his wife moved to Eastham in 1999 and never regretted the move. They love the town and its common. He says:

My wife and I fell in love with Eastham in the early 1990s and moved here full-time in 1999. I love the town common because it marks the gateway to Eastham's wonderful connection to nature, especially the National Seashore around the bend. There are few places on earth where you can watch the sun rise from the ocean in the morning and then watch it set in the same sea at night. People think of Eastham, and Cape Cod in general, as a summer vacation destination but few people from outside the Cape know the beauty here in all four seasons. And the common wears that diversity especially well with flowers emerging in spring, the greens of summer, the colors of fall and the peaceful serenity of winter, especially with a light coating of snow on the windmill.

The thirty-one acre Eastham Historic District, as a whole, is a highly recommended Cape Cod destination, too, for its small village-like vibe and surrounding historic buildings including Eastham Town Hall—a 1912 Colonial Revival structure—and the Eastham Public Library opened in 1898. The Universalist Chapel, situated west of the library, was built in 1889 and features Stick-style architecture, which is a variant of the Queen Anne style. The small structure with wood shingles perfectly matches the look of Cape Cod–style homes. Ruth E. Leistensnider says of the Windmill Park area:

> I spent my summers growing up in Eastham, and the windmill was always a gathering place, especially with the library down the road on Samoset. These days (maybe 40 years later), I find it interesting on the weekends that people stand along the road and hold up signs to support whatever cause they are in favor of at the time. The town common/village green is a place where people can congregate and express their views. It is a democracy, after all, and New England is unique in its Town Meetings to take positions on various issues (such as the Eastham water issuer, which took years to pass at Town Meeting).

The National Register of Historic Places added the Eastham Windmill, as part of the Eastham Center Historic District, to its list in 1999. ◀━

# FALMOUTH

Cape Cod might just be one of the nicest travel destinations in New England with its many fine ocean beaches, sand dunes, seafood restaurants, and enough travel attractions to satisfy every walk of life. While this coastal region brings hundreds of thousands of visitors annually to Massachusetts, one thing is for sure: They generally don't come to see the village greens.

Sure, Cape Cod features a few very nice historic town commons, but it's really the inland towns in Massachusetts that hold the trophy for the best village greens. Falmouth, however, is an exception. This large town with forty-four square miles and seventy-five miles of coastline has somehow held onto its historic preservation anchored by a lovely town green—something to embrace, given that so many inner Cape Cod towns have gone the other way with rampant commercial and residential development.

Visitors to this coastal destination will surely fall in love—hook, line, and sinker—with the triangular town green and the surrounding Falmouth Village Green Historic District. The one-acre town green, bounded by a section of Main Street on the south and north and Hewins Street on the west, offers a truly convenient location in the heart of a vibrant downtown with a seemingly endless and aesthetically pleasing array of shops and restaurants. As a result visitors and locals populate the town green more frequently in the summer. Even though the town common gets more visitors in summer, it doesn't get a lot of use and serves more as a symbol of a typical New England village green, according to Meg Costello, researcher for the Falmouth Museum on the Greens. "It is not used a lot, even during the tour-

**Historic homes surround the Falmouth town green.**

ist season," said Costello. "People do walk individually or as groups through the town common, but the common is more for show. It is a symbol of New England and of our historical downtown."

She adds, "Even if people haven't visited Falmouth before, they are familiar with this type of town common with the grass, American flag flying, and church in the background."

The town green comprises open green space edged with elm and pin oaks and two churches, a bank, and nine two-story houses. Local mid-nineteenth-century businessman icon Elijah Swift planted elms on the town green in 1832 and also built the town common's first two-rail fence. Despite a 1938 hurricane destroying the older elms and a ninety-four-year-old elm removed in 1990 due to Dutch elm disease, the town green today features twenty trees—ten elms, nine pin oaks, and one ginkgo.

A stone dust path traverses the town green from Main and Hewins Streets to the center of the eastern side in front of the First Congregational Church. The American flag flies from its flagpole daily from the middle of the town green with a tricentennial stone time-capsule marker located in front of the pole. A 1930 stone memorial with a wooden wishing well design on top stands at the eastern point.

Not too many events occur on the town green, according to Costello, but one highlight is Christmas decorating and caroling in December. The Falmouth town common also serves as a platform for political viewpoint and social justice gatherings.

Costello says, "The Falmouth town common is still a meeting place," referring to one of the innate historical uses of a Massachusetts town green.

As with most Massachusetts towns and cities, the road to the town green and the community in general is a rather interesting one. First settled by English colonists in 1660 and then incorporated as a town in 1686, Falmouth spent its first century as an agricultural community—most likely enhanced by the area's "rich fish and shellfish resources." Regarding the innate New England relation of town greens and meetinghouses, Falmouth had two meetinghouses built before a third one constructed on the training field—now known as the village green—in 1848. At that time one could see the beginnings of what we know today as the downtown district. A new "village center" evolved when farmland was broken up to make way for tradesmen and sea captains, according to a "National Register of Historic Places nomination for Falmouth Village Green Historic District" document.

In typical New England fashion, most of the well-preserved late-eighteenth- and nineteenth-century residences and institutional buildings are located close to the sidewalk, thus enhancing a more intimate look for the town common area. The wood-frame buildings that surround the town green reflect the early development and evolution of, according to the "National Register of Historic Places nomination for Falmouth Village Green Historic District" document, a "small and isolated colonial seafaring town on the southwest coast of Cape Cod whose people were involved in the historic events of their day." Although certainly no longer a small isolated town that now relies heavily on the vacation industry, one look at these homes validates the authentic historic foundation of the community.

The 1796 First Congregational Church was located on the green, but in 1858 was moved to the north side. Its belfry houses a bell manufactured by Paul Revere!

The district, as a whole, is "significant to the maritime history of Massachusetts and the United States because of the town's long involvement with Charleston, South Carolina, [and] its active participation in the Revolution, the War of 1812, [and] the whaling and live oaking industries," as stated in the "National Register of Historic Places nomination for Falmouth Village Green Historic District" document.

In the finest example of long-standing tradition, the Falmouth town green still features militia drills, parades, and an annual caroling sing-along and Christmas display. When there are no events, the town green remains a central gathering place as a respite from the sometimes-overwhelming summer resort crowds, with buildings at the edge of the town common accommodating antiques shops and upscale commercial ventures. Several historic homes surrounding the town green are now bed-and-breakfasts or inns.

Additionally, the construction of the Queen's Buyway Colonial Revival structure in 1925 created a row of small, one-story stores on Palmer Avenue that not only served as a precursor to modern-day downtown Falmouth shopping, but as a tourist attraction for summer visitors. The town's historical commission and historical society stay open year-round and promote walking tours to allow visitors to gain valuable perspectives on the town's significant and well-preserved history. It's no surprise that the Falmouth Village Green Historic District was added to the National Register of Historic Places in 1996.

While the walkability factor of a town green located right next to so many shopping and dining opportunities is a revelation on Cape Cod, it is indeed the historic aspects that come across most prominently. Strange as it might sound, this appealing combination of modern-day shopping and outstanding historic preservation—wonderfully accented by late Colonial and Federal period buildings—has almost become an anomaly on inner Cape Cod in Barnstable County.

Highly recommended is to walk the town green and stop by the Falmouth Museums on the Green, located right off the common at 55–65 Palmer Avenue (508-548-4857; http://museumsonthegreen .org/visit-us/). According to the website, the museums "contain a treasure trove of stories and artifacts that tell the story of the town of Falmouth, Massachusetts. The museums overlook the Village Green where members of the Colonial militia practiced in the 1700s and sea captains built their homes. Two 18th-century houses display period furniture, fine art, textiles and rotating exhibits that provide a glimpse into the town's rich historic past." Additionally, the museums offer walking tours from June to October and a research library (call ahead, as business hours vary by season).

Consequently, the thriving downtown district, town green, and Falmouth Museums on the Green are definitely, pardon the pun, a "must-sea!"

# FITCHBURG

Part of a local historic district, Fitchburg's oval-shaped Upper Common serves as a great respite in the middle of a small but densely populated north-central Massachusetts city. Initially, the land for Upper Common was deeded to the First Parish Church (which sits at the head of the common) in 1882. Back in 1762 the land extended all the way down to the former city hall, but has been shortened quite a bit to a few acres. Today, however, the welcoming appeal of a truly attractive Massachusetts town green serves as a much-needed respite from the surrounding urban elements. Transforming from an agricultural community to an industrial one necessitated that need.

The town green—an Olmsted Brothers–designed landscape—offers a water fountain with several sculptures by Fitchburg native Herbert Adams, benches, and a gazebo. The *Boys and the Turtles* statue, created by Adams, was finished in 1889. Also on the town green is a 1960-created dedication stone to Arthur Longsjo, a famous Olympic athlete from Fitchburg, and a 1928 statue of an angel that commemorates World War II soldiers. The Rollstone Boulder (a big tourist attraction and treasure to the city that can be visited when at the Upper Common) was finished in November 1930. The tiny park around the boulder is called Litchfield Park. Renaissance Park (another little memorial park just below the Upper Common at 960 Main Street) was finished June 28, 1929. Additionally, there's a stone on the Upper Common recognizing President Calvin Coolidge, who visited the town green on November 12, 1928.

By now—just by hearing the description of the Upper Common—you have come to realize that Fitchburg has quite a history. It certainly

**Inviting benches and a brick walkway lead to the *Boys and the Turtles* statue and the First Parish Church.**

does! Before a Native American presence, European settlement began in 1719 when Fitchburg was known as South Town. The community became incorporated as Lunenburg in 1728, but in 1764 the western section of Lunenburg was "set off as a separate town called Fitchburg and the new town's first meetinghouse was built soon after in 1766," according to the 2006 Massachusetts Heritage Landscape Inventory Program. The city's unique steep rocky terrain and mix of pine and walnut forests did not make for an exactly ideal agricultural center—unlike so many surrounding towns—so eventually Fitchburg turned into an industrial giant starting around 1760. Located on the Nashua

River, Fitchburg started with a gristmill, then saw and textile mills, and then a paper mill (1803). It also was home to the Fitchburg Cotton Manufacturing Corporation (1807) and other businesses that produced chairs and scythe and edge tools, as well as machine shops, according to the Massachusetts Heritage Landscape Inventory Program. Fitchburg also became a significant "railroad town," but that and many industries began to dissolve in the 1920s.

Despite many hardships since the 1920s, Fitchburg remains, in many ways, a proud city with many of the elements that make urban areas great—museums, a college (Fitchburg State University), fine tree-lined neighborhoods with wonderfully kept historic homes, a good dining scene, and examples of excellent historical preservation.

The Upper Common is certainly one of those well-preserved areas. Just a look around the parklike grounds confirms that greatness, according to the Massachusetts Heritage Landscape Inventory Program, as it is

> bordered by many important resources such as the Fitchburg City Hall (718 Main Street, 1852); the Calvinistic Congregational Church, now called Faith United Parish (820 Main Street, 1896, NR), designed by Henry M. Francis in the Richardsonian Romanesque style; the Swedish Congregational Church (Rollstone Street, 1893), also designed by Francis; the Universalist Church (840–850 Main Street, 1847–1848), a Greek Revival building that now is in commercial use; Old Town Hall/Second Meetinghouse (900–904 Main Street, 1796, moved here ca. 1836), now in commercial use; the First Parish Unitarian Universalist Church (on Upper Common, 1837); the Swedish Emanuel Lutheran Evangelical Church (1 Caldwell Street, 1896).

Many events take place on the Upper Common, including summer concerts on the common, a Veteran's Day service downtown at Monument Park (but not directly on the common), a December tree-lighting ceremony, and the First Parish Church drum circle on the first Thursday of every month. The park is located at the intersection of Main, Mechanic, and Prospect Streets near the Rollstone Boulder.

Finally, Katrina Brown, of the Fitchburg Historical Society, shares a rather interesting Upper Common anecdote that took place in August 2015. Katrina, on her routine walk from the Historical Society to the Fitchburg Post Office, noticed on her way back a large group of people forming to one side of the town green.

She made her way through the crowd of approximately seventy-five and asked why everyone congregated together. Somebody pointed to a baby moose that was stuck in an adjacent backyard.

"It was a great juxtaposition of city and nature," says Brown. "We are near the Nashua River and the moose must have made his way down!"

# FOXBOROUGH

Bailey Falls, the fictional town in the classic movie *It's a Wonderful Life*—which focuses on the togetherness of people and their resolve in a small town—has absolutely nothing on Foxborough and its town common.

Foxborough is truly a lifelong story of a "town, its people, their common," as local historian and former Foxborough reporter-editor Jack Authelet likes to say. He wrote a brilliant analysis in 2012 with that title (featured in the Foxborough Annual Report) that tells a wonderful story of a truly great close-knit American town.

Back in the mid-seventeenth century, residents discovered an innate connection to each other, thus necessitating a desire to separate from being residents of towns like Walpole, Wrentham, and Stoughton and the former community of Stoughtonham, according to Authelet. Nothing against those towns, mind you, but the sense of community was already well in place and the quest for community independence became a way of life.

Following the unwavering New England book of steadfast rules, the requirement to incorporate involved having a meetinghouse and hiring a minister. Authelet says that three residents offered land at the location of three roads at what is now the Foxborough town common and that citizens saved their money and built their own meetinghouse in 1763. Foxborough became incorporated as a town in 1778, but growing expenses resulted in the building being torn down in 1822 when Congregationalists erected its church on the land.

So, what does this have to do with a town common other than being located in the general vicinity? The three residents had originally

**The locally famous Foxborough sign resides on the beautiful town green.**

promised to make land available if the town did become incorporated. The conveyance of the land was offered to Josiah Pratt, Aaron Everett, and Nathan Clark, then selectmen of the Town of Foxborough, "and to their successors in said town forever" according to Authelet. A quick claim deed on May 19, 1853, was successful, thus transferring the title for the land to Foxborough. Lot grading, a single rail fence to encircle the area, tree planting, and a cistern dug out at the foot of the lot helped create a template of an oasis that remains to this very day. Of course even back then the residents foot the bill, contributing anywhere from fifty cents to fifty dollars.

Soon, further beautification of the town common elevated to the next level when, Authelet says, local businessmen formed a private group, the Sylvanian Association, and through the vote of Foxborough residents on April 6, 1857, proceeded to "ornament, grade and enclose the Common." Gone were the shrubs, trees, and rocks in lieu of a finer landscape as well as the road that ran straight through the area connecting Main and Central Streets. This community template has endured to this very day, with residents always finding a way to donate to the maintenance and improvement of the town common.

The Foxborough town common did experience a few bumps in the road but always found a solution. Nothing represents that town common community spirit better than when the population had virtually doubled in the 1960s, cars became longer, curbs shorter, and the fence being chipped away by the impact of cars parking. That cast-iron fence deteriorated so greatly that it could not be repaired. Authelet, then editor of the *Foxboro Reporter* and a disciple of the Sylvanian business model, helped avert tax money being used to repair the fence by seeking public donations through an article in his paper. When a banker who shared the responsibility of this incentive opened the bank one day, he found a huge line waiting to give money!

First in line, according to Authelet, was "the late Betty Morse who remembered her husband Howard lifting her over the fence in their courting days to attend events on the Common. They had collected quarters for many years and she felt the Common Fence effort would be a most appropriate donation."

Authelet reports that "the entire community became caught up in the effort. The Jaycee Wives had a fashion show. The Young Life group at Bethany Church held a paper drive while children on Villa Drive set up a refreshment stand. The Foxborough State Hospital employees took up a collection, the Foxborough Historical Society held a flea market, and members of the Fire Department made a donation as did many businesses." Local businessman Jerry Rodman shared proceeds from the parking lot on Route 1 in use for stadium events.

As funds poured in, Archie Hanna, a local craftsman and water commissioner, hinted he might be able to make the pattern for a section of common fence, according to Authelet. Making epoxy molds of some of the intricate sections, fashioning other parts from wood and other materials, "he reproduced the exact shape of the fence that would be impressed into a box of sand at the foundry to make a cavity into which molten metal could be poured to form the section. His pattern was a few inches over-size to allow for shrinkage when cooling," states Authelet.

Clearly Foxborough residents have always loved their town common. Since 1857 the town green has been a social gathering place, and today is no exception with its Thursday evening summer Concerts on the Common, tree-lighting ceremony and caroling during the holiday season, Jaycees yard sales, the McGinty Family Fun Day the Saturday closest to September 11, a theater program where kids perform plays on the town common, and a Memorial Day observance at the foot of the common.

Gillette Stadium—home of the New England Patriots football team—and the adjacent Patriot Place might seem like the focal point of Foxborough, but nothing could be further from the truth.

Away from all the bright lights is a "real" town, steeped in history and New England charm. Drive a few miles to the town center, and the circular town common stands, above and beyond, as the most notable attraction with its wide hilly land and huge Foxborough sign. The town green contains war memorials, a centennial marker, police memorial, firefighters memorial, a bandstand, and beautiful open space in the center of Foxborough. But it is the locals who bring their town common to the next level, for without them, the spirit of this town would not be so apparent during town green gatherings and, in general, across the whole town.

# FRANKLIN

Many think of Franklin as a small town, but technically this southwest Boston suburb is incorporated as a city—and one that is filled with a tremendous sense of history. The Franklin Public Library, located right off the beautiful town common, might be the city's best historical representation, as it is the first freestanding public library in the country, dating back to 1790. After the town of Exeter changed its name to Franklin in honor of Dr. Benjamin Franklin, the US statesman, publisher, scientist, social activist, patriot, legislator, and all-around American historical icon decided to donate some of his favorite books to the Franklin townsfolk in 1778, as a token of appreciation of the locals naming their town after him. Imagine that, a Founding Father showing gratitude toward a little New England town that couldn't hold a Colonial candle, historically, to nearby Boston or Lexington and Concord! In 1790, the books found a home, as Franklin town meeting members voted to lend books to residents free of charge, thus creating the first public library in the United States. To this very day you can see the collection housed in an antique wooden cabinet in the Franklin Public Library.

While the Franklin Public Library earns "top booking" as a Franklin attraction at the town common, the town green, itself, is also a major player in the city's charm. Located on 5.5 acres, the wedge-shaped Franklin Town Common is filled with mature oak and maple trees providing wonderful shade, sculptural cast-concrete and wood-slat park benches, well-maintained crisscrossing walkways made with large-aggregate concrete, a brick gazebo bandstand dating back

**The 5.5-acre Franklin town green serves as a relaxing place to walk.**

to 1917, sixteen classical iron lampposts, two flagpoles, and nine war memorials.

"I consider the common as the 'heart and soul' of Franklin," says Franklin resident Helen Chaulk, who lives next to the common. "It's a great place where the whole town (city) regularly comes together for festive fun, but also for more serious occasions like the Memorial Day parade and remembrance service for our lost servicemen."

Eileen Burnard adds, "The Franklin Common is my panacea. It is where I come for respite and peace. I walk with my dog and always meet someone new. We walk till tired and sit when weary under the graceful arches of the trees. Such a wonderful place."

The octagonal bandstand is truly an eye catcher with its Far East-meets-Craftsman style. The detail is truly special, described in Franklin's National Register of Historic Places nomination application:

> Measuring approximately 30 feet wide by 20 feet tall, [the bandstand] rests on a brick and granite base. Piers of thin smooth tile alternating with rough brick rise to support a broad octahedral hip roof covered with red tiles. The unpainted underside of the roof rests on carved wooden corbels and large wooden brackets. An iron balustrade encloses the deck of the rotunda, which is reached by a set of six steps on the south side. A circular motif designed into the deck reads: PRESENTED TO THE TOWN OF FRANKLIN BY HARRY TAFT HAYWARD AND EDITH WIRES HAYWARD—MCMXVII. In 1983, the bandstand was re-bricked and the roof repaired by students at the Tri-County School with funding from the town. In 1995, Clark, Cutler and McDermott Company renovated the structure.

One of the town common's finest features, located at its north end, is a beautiful garden maintained by the Franklin Garden Club. Planted with low-growing shrubs and flowers that flank a path leading to monuments commemorating World Wars I and II and the Korean War, this area is one of the most visited in the historic district. The respect for honoring military who have protected our country's freedoms is exemplary and should be used as a model for any New England town common looking to potentiate their central historic districts. Monuments include the Civil War Soldiers' Monument (1903), The G.A.R. Memorial Boulder (1913, to honor the preservation of the Union), and the World War I Monument.

The Civil War Soldiers' Monument is particularly impressive—made completely of blue granite—rising twenty-one feet from a seven-foot-square, three-part base to a tall pedestal supporting a seven-foot, six-inch figure of a volunteer Union soldier.

There's also a unique-looking Spanish–American War Monument paying tribute to the 1898 war to free Cuba from Spanish domination.

Suzanne Marak used to live across the street from the Franklin town common and has nothing but warm memories. "I have many fond memories of living across from the Franklin town common, or green," says Marak. "My young children played there. My older ones romanced there, my daughter had her wedding pictures taken on the town common, my husband and I used to walk around it. I, through the years, found many reasons to sit on a bench and daydream or read or relax on the town common. It was always such a pretty picture looking out my kitchen window, any season, any year."

St. Mary's Church—the largest suburban Catholic parish in the Boston Archdiocese with some fifteen thousand members—resides as the most prominent historic structure at the town green. With a dramatic yet inviting Gothic Revival style and a rectory with Georgian Revival influences complemented with Tudor Revival decorative motifs and a red brick and limestone rectory, the St. Mary's layout represents a memorable, prototypical town green area church as well as any in the state.

Homes in the common area and historic district, as a whole, look like something out of a *Who's Who in Architectural Home Styles* with Federal, Greek Revival, Italianate, Second Empire, Victorian Gothic, Queen Anne, Colonial Revival, Tudor, and Craftsman styles all represented. Most of the homes were built in the mid- to late-nineteenth century, although several late-eighteenth-century dwellings exist— and, generally, are in fine shape.

Dean College, dating back to 1865, is virtually steps away from the town green and adds a nice college-town touch with its historic large main building that dates from 1874.

Franklin is an extremely close-knit community and prides itself on town common events including the town's Fourth of July celebration, summer concerts and farmers' market on the common, and the annual Holiday Lighting on the Common. The Fourth of July might be the most prominent event, with food booths, amusements, musical entertainment, a laser-light show, and children's parade.

Whatever the event or other reason to visit the Franklin town common, memories abound for those lucky enough to soak in this true New England experience—then, now, and forever.

Shannon Reynolds says:

I love my Franklin town common because it is a central piece of my "old Franklin." For me, it still reminds me of when I was very little (almost forty years ago) and saw a police horse for the first time, likely for some town event, and getting to pet the horse and talk to the policeman. It also reminds me of enjoying myself at a Franklin Fire Department town fire drill exhibition over twenty years ago. Watching the fireman put on a show of the work they do while so many of us stood around in awe. And finally, for years, my favorite stop was the Fourth of July weekend celebration to see the community together.

# GRAFTON

If you are looking to travel to classic small town Vermont without ever leaving the Worcester area, the Grafton Town Common will surely satisfy. This scenic three-acre green space with paths coming from multiple directions dates back to 1738 and is surrounded by historical homes and buildings (mostly from the mid-nineteenth century) including the Grafton Inn (1805) that has been serving meals and offering accommodations since its inception, as well as the Grafton Country Store (1806 with origins dating back to 1733), the Italianate Unitarian Church (1863), and the Greek Revival Congregational Church (1833). Monuments memorialize the Civil War and World War I soldiers lost in those two wars who were from Grafton.

With its rich history, the town green and surrounding area are part of the 1981-designated Grafton Common Historic District. Although the town common has gone from about eight acres to around three due to expansion of the railroad industry, the well-defined look of the circular green makes it an obvious and locally famous destination as a classic Massachusetts town common. The district was also added to the National Register of Historic Places in 1988.

One of the more remarkable stories centering around the town green: The common features a handsome bandstand that was built by Hollywood moviemakers Metro-Goldwyn-Mayer for a scene in the 1935 movie *Ah Wilderness*. Written by the legendary Eugene O'Neill and made for the silver screen, *Ah Wilderness* stars Mickey Rooney, Wallace Beery, Lionel Barrymore, Cecilia Parker, and Aline MacMahon. It's a story about small town life in turn-of-the-twentieth-century

**A bandstand constructed for a 1930s Hollywood movie and the historic Grafton Inn create a quintessential New England look.**

America, and a young boy's problems facing adolescence, according to the IMDb website.

Linda Casey, of the Grafton Historical Society, reports that the movie "was the biggest thing to ever happen on the town common. It was Hollywood coming to our small town. The movie stars would have lemonade and cookies with the locals. A Grafton resident who has since passed on told me a few years ago about what it was like to see some of these stars without makeup. It was quite different than what people perceived stars to look like!"

More than two hundred Grafton residents participated in the filming as extras, according to a 1985 article in the *Blackstone Valley Tribune*.

Happily, the bandstand remains today as a prominent part of the Grafton town green, although it has gone through some extensive renovations through the years. The town green, as a whole, was established in 1738, coinciding with the building of a meetinghouse—a significant requirement for a Massachusetts town to be officially incorporated. The town green is a beauty, enclosed by an 1845 fence built out of granite posts and wooden rails, according to Casey.

Grafton's history clearly goes back well before the 1930s, however, as its origins can be traced back to when the area was an Indian praying village with its own state-recognized reservation known as Hassanamessit until 1637, when the Reverend John Elliot converted the Nipmuc tribe to Christianity. Eventually Europeans would settle the area in 1724, leading to its official incorporation in 1735.

The Grafton Historical Society states that the original forty proprietors of Grafton voted that land from the Hassanamessit Plantation would be set aside as a town common. Soon, in 1738, locals would establish a town green and meetinghouse, burial ground, schoolhouse, and militia training field all on the property. The first meetinghouse of the Congregational Puritan settlement was built in 1730 and stood at the center of the common for approximately one hundred years. In 1845, Grafton locals fenced, graded, and planted with trees the land, setting up the area for a look that can be enjoyed to this very day, states the Grafton Historical Society.

Besides serving as a movie location, another unlikely scenario grew out of the town common area as shoe factories situated themselves there in the 1800s before the Industrial Revolution, according to Casey. The shoe factories specialized in work boots before the industry located down south. It's hard to believe in such a rural-looking town with agricultural leanings that tiny Grafton was second in Massachusetts only to Lynn in the shoe-manufacturing business. Other areas of Grafton had been well established as major players in the Industrial Revolution's mill-factory growth, but the shoe factories near the center never became a central part of our current-day common historical knowledge of this Worcester suburb.

Today, any factory presence is virtually gone, while the pastoral village green offers myriad seasonal events like the Memorial Day observance at the foot of the common, the farmers' market on Thursday during the summer, Grafton History Day in May, summer community concerts, ice-cream socials, plant sales, the Congregational Church's Harvest Fair in September, and a Santa visit during the holidays, where lights on the trees lend additional quintessential New England ambiance.

It's truly astonishing that driving just ten minutes from Worcester—the second-most populated city in New England—leads to this quiet, hilltop village within a semi-rural town that seems miles away from civilization.

# GREENFIELD

A lively small city with an unmistakable "Main Street USA look," Greenfield prides itself on a great diversity of independently owned businesses. Let's start, however, with the welcoming town green before examining thriving Main Street and the other components that make downtown Greenfield so appealing in this foothill of the Berkshires of Western Massachusetts community.

Greenfield residents laid out the town common in 1749 when Greenfield was still a part of Deerfield. Over time, virtually all sectors of Greenfield—including animals—have used the town green for some kind of activity. Initially, firefighters drew water on the town common to fight fires, according to Massachusetts Department of Conservation and Recreation's 2009 "Greenfield Reconnaissance Report." Additionally, horses drank from a town green trough. Before the famous Franklin County Fair that started in 1848, county fairs were held on the town common. Since the 1920s, a wonderful tradition of decorating the common with ice sculpture for the Greenfield Winter Carnival remains just as popular as ever. The town green also plays host every Christmas season to the city's nativity scene. The Saturday Farmers' Market—going back to 1975—also takes place on the town common on Saturday during the warm weather seasons. In addition, the Noon Lunchtime Concert Series remains a local favorite in the summer.

A monument from 1870 prominently remains on the town green to honor Greenfield residents who fought and died in the Civil War.

Solid-looking municipal buildings form the town common, also known as Court Square, frame the town green, along with many other historically significant structures (including several banks and a post

**The Greenfield Farmers' Market takes place on a cool, crisp fall day at Greenfield's Court Square.**

office from 1915) from the Federal Period to the 1930s. The Leavitt-Hovy house (Greenfield Public Library)—a short walk from the town green—is an architectural gem listed on the National Register of Historic Places. It was originally built in 1797 by famous architect Asher Benjamin for a local judge, but Greenfield purchased the home in 1907 as a home for the Greenfield Public Library. These buildings and the town common are all part of the Main Street Historic District that include several blocks of Main Street extending roughly from Chapman Street in the west to Franklin Street in the east, as well as a number of properties facing the common along Bank Row, south of Main Street.

The Garden Movie Theater (listed on the National Register of Historic Places); book, furniture, and music stores (used record and instruments, respectively); barber and tailor shops; and the Greenfield Farmers' Market certainly tip the unique downtown look in the right direction, but what really sets apart this small western Massachusetts city of approximately seventeen thousand residents from virtually any community in the United States is the presence of a full-service department store. Wilson's, right in the heart of the increasingly vibrant downtown and virtually right across the street from the town green, will take you back to another place and time—a family-owned and operated business dating back to the 1880s with twenty departments on four floors. From men's and women's clothing departments to toys and a candy counter, for starters, Wilson's combines a nostalgic feeling with modern-day retail practicality.

One of only a handful of family-owned department stores left in America, Wilson's will warm your heart as an American retail treasure that not only focuses on a terrific variety of merchandise, but also pride of ownership and wonderful customer service that you just don't see much of anymore in today's rather lethargic world of hired retail help. You could complete all your Christmas shopping here, and also see Santa (as well as the Easter Bunny in the spring) along the way—and feel wonderful about the whole experience. Free parking, lack of a hectic mall scene, and the presence of a wholesome, friendly retail personality certainly help the cause.

Greenfield is certainly a rising star among small Massachusetts cities with a proud historic past and a good sense of modern-day revitalization and preservation, and it all starts at the town green!

# GROTON

Groton, officially settled and incorporated in 1655, has a special place in many a New Englander's heart. The friendly quaint downtown, beautiful historic homes, farmland, scenic public conservation spaces, biking and walking trails, welcoming hills and valleys, and nearby apple-picking farms make this small north-central Massachusetts town a favorite among those who love the pure, unspoiled side of Massachusetts travel. It's especially beautiful in the fall when the foliage colors typically become brilliant and the crisp chill in the air make for an ideal country bike ride or a rustling through the leaves on a sidewalk.

For many, the Groton town common serves as a prime town landmark, a group meeting place for those traveling the region, and a memorable snapshot of quintessential New England. Located on a hilly section of the downtown district, the Groton town common in front of the First Parish Church possesses an important historical presence as an assembly area in 1775 for Minutemen who fought in the Battle of Lexington and Concord.

The green grass with pleasing shade from trees serves as an unofficial outdoor welcoming center for Groton, but also noteworthy is the First Parish's history and awe-inspiring structure.

The first Parish building was constructed in 1666 in another part of town when the area was known as Groton Plantation. The Parish served as Groton's first meetinghouse but was, unfortunately, burned by Indians during the King Philip's War in 1676. This present church, built in 1755, is the Parish's fourth building and the second on this site, according to the First Parish of Groton. Groton served as the county seat from 1776 to 1787, where the Courts of General

**The First Parish Church illuminates the town green at night.**

Sessions and of Common Plea for Middlesex County sat in this meetinghouse.

Today the Groton town common differs from many others of this genre in Massachusetts by minimizing seasonal events. The church features an Easter egg hunt during the Easter season that is open to the public and holds some yard sales. Holiday tree decorating takes place during December.

Julie Skowranek, of the First Parish, says that the church holds an annual event inside that has ties to the town green. "At the end of May, we have in the church, an 'Alive at 75' annual event where middle schoolers hold a town meeting," says Skowranek. "Town meetings go way back in our history!"

The First Parish website has this beautifully written section on the nuances of the Church:

Francis Ridgeway created the town clock in the belfry and placed [it] in position in 1809. The Paul Revere bell was cast in 1819 and has been in use since then. The clock and bell are still wound by the Keeper of the Clock twice a week. The interior of the church was altered again in 1877 but later partly restored in 1916. Practically none of the original interior survives. In 1986 following the rebuilding of the foundation, the church was recognized by the Massachusetts Historical Commission as an historic structure. The church communion silver consists of nineteen pieces, many being gifts of members. Most of this is now at the Boston Museum of Fine Arts, where it is occasionally on display. In 1891 the present Hook and Hastings organ, built in 1876, was obtained from The Church of the Advent on Beacon Hill in Boston. The lovely old home next to the Church on Powder House Road was the parsonage for the minister but presently is used as a parish house for church school classes, offices, and meetings.

# HARDWICK

The Hardwick Village Historic District, placed on the National Register of Historic Places in 1991, features a lovely traditional New England town green within a sleepy setting bordered by Petersham, Barre, Greenwich, Ruggles Hill, and Gilbertville Roads. Like many rural towns in the central western Massachusetts area, the town common area shows no commercial offerings, as of this writing, and the strong traditional New England presence of three white churches and inviting old homes. The town green is almost triangular in shape and split by road with two parcels of land. The look of this historic district is quite different than other areas of Hardwick, which are rural and with industrial lineage.

"We're such a small town that you can't miss the town common," laughs Emily Bancroft, of the Hardwick Historical Society. "Hardwick is made up on several different villages, so the other parts of town don't have anything that looks like the town center."

The pride and joy of the town common is the Hardwick Community Fair, typically held the third weekend in August. Originated in 1762 (Hardwick was incorporated in 1739), this is the oldest community fair in the United States, and one, to this very day, completely run by volunteers. While locals saturate this revered traditional event, many travel great distances, also, to enjoy the Colonial-style country fair featuring many free and inexpensive activities.

Fay Butler, president of the Hardwick Community Fair, describes a typical event:

> It is a traditional Colonial-style country fair with an agricultural theme . . . The Common has a variety of activities; many free and

**The Hardwick town green takes on a fall foliage personality.**

others inexpensive, bringing together a blend of old and new. It's a family event where children can enjoy themselves and so can their parents, without emptying their pockets. Check out the Kids Only . . . like the Frog Jumping Competition. Other buildings around the Common display art, photography, and crafts created by local folks. The Old Town Hall has displays of baked goods, flowers, and vegetables, all competing for the illusive Blue Ribbon. The Fair culminates in an auction of all perishable exhibits, where even "Aunt Mable's Blue Ribbon-winning blueberry cake" goes to the highest bidder.

While the Hardwick town common is revered by its residents as a symbol of the town's beautiful traditional New England look, there are not many other events happening here other than a Sunday farmers' market during the spring and early fall.

# HARVARD

Driving, walking, or biking down the hill from Route 111 south into the center of Harvard evokes that proverbial feeling of visiting grandmother's house in the country—you know, over the meadow and through the woods. A truly cozy small Nashua Valley town, at the eastern edge of Worcester County, Harvard is known for farms (some offering apple picking in the fall) and long winding country roads. The central district—added to the National Register of Historic Places in 1997—looks just like one would expect in small town New England. Old homes, municipal buildings, the nearby Fruitlands Museum (celebrating art, nature, and history), former churches that mostly post-date 1831, and the Harvard General Store encompass a small and larger town common. The larger town common space—popular among locals, Central Massachusetts travelers, and bikers passing through—is simply a lovely place to stop, unwind, and take in a truly traditional New England town.

Like many old New England towns, the town green section of Harvard has served as the central town meeting point, in this case, since Harvard's incorporation in 1732. This includes the majority of civic and religious buildings and commerce—today, in the form of the Harvard General Store and a few service-oriented businesses. The Massachusetts Cultural Resource System website states that the Harvard town green area features about twenty homes that were built before 1831. Buildings from that period of time have generally disappeared due to newer development, but we are not talking exactly modern here. In the late-nineteenth and early-twentieth centuries, Harvard added "a new town hall, replaced its church, added a Cath-

**The Harvard town common starts out level but leads to a church on the hill.**

olic church, and built a large new store," according to the Massachusetts Cultural Resource Information System.

Events on the town green include a tree-lighting ceremony that usually takes place the second weekend in December; Concerts on the Common at the Unitarian Universalist Church at selected times throughout the year; the Ayer Rotary Club's Apple Blossom Festival—a "Town Day," of sorts—held the Saturday prior to Mother's Day; and myriad cultural, artistic, and educational events at the Center on the Common within the Hapgood Library (see http://centeronthecommon.org/sample-page/for event listings).

Just up the road is the Fruitlands Museum, which features art, nature, and historical exhibitions. Founded in 1914 by Clara Endicott

Sears, the Fruitlands was once an experimental Utopian Community spearheaded by Bronson Alcott and Charles Lane at this location in 1843. The Fruitlands website, at www.fruitlands.org/museum-history, states that the campus includes the following:

- The Fruitlands Farmhouse, the site of an experiment in communal living led by Alcott and Lane in 1843
- The Shaker Museum, home to the largest archive of Harvard Shaker documents in the world
- The Native American Gallery, which houses a significant collection of artifacts that honor the spiritual presence and cultural history of the first Americans
- The Art Gallery, containing one hundred Hudson River School landscape paintings and, significantly, over 230 nineteenth-century vernacular portraits, the second-largest collection in the country. The Art Gallery also hosts a variety of rotating exhibits throughout the year.

# HOPKINTON

The Hopkinton town common looks like a lot of other small town greens in Massachusetts, with its gazebo, paved walkways, benches, memorial sites and historical statues, large expansive lawn, and church in the background of a classic New England scene.

One trait, however, helps differentiate the Hopkinton town common from the rest in New England, or any other part of the United States, for that matter: The village green is the start of the world-famous Boston Marathon. On the Monday of Patriots Day weekend in April, thousands gather in and around the town common to be part of a race that spans 26.2 miles east to Boston. The marathon dates back to 1924 and has transformed from a small happening to a global event—the oldest annual running race in the United States. There's even a Boston Marathon "Starter" statue (see photo on following page) on the town green, dedicated to Hopkinton resident George Brown (1880 to 1937) who served as a starter at the Boston Marathon for twenty-four years!

The beautiful Veteran's Memorial Gazebo—a familiar sight for those watching the start of the Boston Marathon on television—is, interestingly enough, not part of the historical fabric of the town green (although it certainly has a historic look). The gazebo was built in 1988 for about fifteen thousand dollars from donations made to the War Memorial Building Fund and other sponsors that helped create the new bandstand. Some of the events that employ the gazebo include summer concerts, weddings, Memorial and Veteran's Day celebrations, and December holiday festivities.

**This statue honors Hopkinton resident George Brown, who served as a starter at the Boston Marathon.**

While virtually all Massachusetts town commons have a special story to tell, the Hopkinton Town Common finishes as one of the most interesting. It's hard to believe, in retrospect, that this pastoral location in a small town has gained such fame because of a running race.

With a National Register of Historic Places designation that includes twenty-three properties, the look of the Hopkinton Historic District is pure New England—admirable given the significant expanse of commercial and modern residential development that has saturated the Route 495 belt. Incorporated in 1715, agriculture served as the main industry until 1840, when shoe manufacturing took over as a main industry. Shoe manufacturing is long gone from Hopkinton, and the town now mainly serves as a bedroom community to Boston and Worcester. It is the town common district, however, that greatly helps Hopkinton hold onto its historic look—and what a look it is, perhaps representing traditional New England as well as any town in Massachusetts.

Whether visiting the Hopkinton town common on Boston Marathon Day or on a much more quiet day, you will, no doubt, feel like a part of traditional New England. The village green is a way of life in this neck of the woods and forever shall be a traditional gathering place. It's just that our Colonial forefathers probably never could have imagined a gathering of this magnitude at a Massachusetts town green, although perhaps any visionary and telepathic folks living around the mid-1800s had this thought "run through their minds" when Hopkinton served as a major shoe-manufacturing town!

# IPSWICH

The small, quaint-looking 1820 Little Red House—also known as the Hall-Haskell House and the current-day Ipswich Visitor Center—suggests a sense of history to anyone visiting or passing through this coastal North Shore town. Very few people know, however, the history runs so deep that Ipswich features more seventeenth-century "First Period" colonial homes than any other community in the country, according to the Ipswich Visitor Center website (www.ipswichvisitorcenter.org/).

Many of those fine homes surround the South Green and side streets to make up the area known as the South Green Historic District. The homes include Georgian, Federal, and Greek Revival styles, some are Victorians, and there are also Colonial styles of architecture represented.

The district actually features two separate town greens—one by the Little Red House and the other just over the Choate Bridge (the oldest stone bridge in the country!) right at the First Church located on the appropriately named One Meetinghouse Green on Route 1A. The green near the church has a higher concentration of history and remains true to form, with its historical template not appearing that much different than what historians know the common looked like in 1834. Following the tenets of a Massachusetts town green, the present day First Church was first a meetinghouse until separation of church and state changed all that. The First Church, however, still calls itself a "meetinghouse," but in a twenty-first-century way. The modern-day meetinghouse centers on, according to the church website, "groups such as AA, the local library, a dance class, yoga class, business associ-

**Ipswich honors those who served our country.**

ation, wedding receptions, etc." The sanctuary also is used for musical events and recitals and houses a nursery school.

Ipswich—founded by John Winthrop (son of John Winthrop, one of the founders of the Massachusetts Bay Colony in 1630 and its first governor, elected in England in 1629)—established the South Green in 1686. Cattle gathered here before being located to outlying pastures, men met here for military training, and education took place. For a while South Green was known as School House Green, led by Ezekiel Cheever, a well-known New England educator who came to Ipswich in 1650 as schoolmaster. The town established a grammar school in 1636 and moved to the South Green. The school moved again, off the common in 1794, thus taking the "education center" association away from the town green, although still located in the South Green Historic District.

The South Green Historic District was added to the National Register of Historic Places in 1980. A great way to learn more about the district is to visit the Ipswich Visitor Center (open seven days a week, 9 a.m. to 5 p.m., Memorial Day weekend through mid-October) at 36 South Main Street (978-356-8540), or the Ipswich Museum (founded in 1890) at 54 South Main Street, (978-356-2811, www.ipswichmuseum.org/). The museum is anchored by the 1677 Whipple House and the 1800 Heard House.

Events happening at the Ipswich town greens include a tree-lighting ceremony by the First Church, farmers' markets during the summer on Wednesday afternoon, and occasional summer concerts. ◀━

# LAWRENCE

During the mid-1800s, the Lawrence Common was planned as a passive open-space Victorian promenade garden as a respite from urban life in one of the Northeast's most important industrial textile cities. That initial vision of community planning for this lovely park remains strongly intact.

As part of a grid layout in the fabulous North Common Historic District (and on the National Register of Historic Places), the Lawrence Town Common stands as the second-largest city green in Massachusetts—next to the Boston Common—coming in at 17.5 acres. The common's size is certainly impressive on its own, but the story behind its creation and its one-of-a-kind nuances elevate the Lawrence Common to Massachusetts town common greatness!

In 1848 the Essex Company gave the City of Lawrence the land to serve, as previously mentioned, as an oasis in the middle of a bustling industrial city. Before that the land produced nothing more than a sand heap and swamp—and other parts were sown with buckwheat, and one corner was a cabbage patch—according to a January 2012 article in the *Lawrence Eagle Tribune.*

Charles Storrow—chief engineer at the Essex Company, a company organized to harness the water power of the Merrimack River—created the basic design of the Lawrence Common. His grandson James Storrow, by the way, was a Boston-area lawyer and investment banker and had the city's Storrow Drive named after him! Interestingly, there is a link between the grid layout of Boston's Back Bay and Lawrence's similar layout. Additionally, Harvard University names like Lowell House, Lawrence Hall, and Appleton Chapel clearly have

**Historic buildings surround Lawrence Common.**

a nexus to the Lawrence area—no surprise given James Storrow attended Harvard University in Cambridge (the city borders Boston)!

During the creation of the Lawrence Town Common and Historic District, the Essex Company eliminated 6.7 miles of rocks and trees, while putting brooks underground to create the blueprint of the city's new heart and soul, according to Jonas A. Stundzia, city historian and chairman of the Lawrence Historical Commission.

With Storrow setting the foundation for the Lawrence Common, the city then brought in Frederic Law Olmsted as a design star to create the Victorian Promenade-style of the town green that, to this very day, has a timeless appeal. It's interesting to note that the Victorian style wasn't exactly Olmsted's cup of tea, but the City of Lawrence knew they had a master on their hands and that he also happened to be an expert in dealing with problematic water tables—an issue Lawrence experienced in parts of the open land.

Stundzia says that during the early days of the Lawrence Town Common, the presence of a massive line of elm trees planted in 1850 provided further beauty to the open land.

"It was like walking in a jungle," says Stundzia.

The trees, unfortunately, succumbed to Dutch elm disease, starting in 1918, thus eradicating an attractive element of the Lawrence Common. The Lawrence Common nevertheless stayed true to its original vision, offering a beautiful open space for residents to enjoy. The green did run into some maintenance problems during the 1970s, however, when the decline of local industries had a deleterious effect on the city as a whole.

"Fortunately, placement on the National Register of Historic Places gave the area some legs," says Stundzia, and the Lawrence Town Common's temporarily lost attractive looks came back.

The Lawrence Town Common is known today, by many, as Compagnone Park, although the common's original moniker holds near and dear to the hearts among longtime residents, historians, and other traditionalists. The Compagnone brothers of Lawrence gave their lives during World War II.

The common features many memorials and monuments in dedication to those who served and paid the ultimate price for defending our freedoms. The 1881 Civil War memorial lists the names of Lawrence men who fought for the Union. The green also showcases World War II, Spanish–American War, Gulf War, and Korean War memorials.

Modern-day amenities: a fenced baseball field with a dugout and spectator seating; the Robert Frost Fountain for scenery and relaxation across from Lawrence City Hall; and a playground on the Jackson Street side with a slide, swings, a jungle gym, and monkey bars.

For added historical authenticity, many civic buildings face the town green including "late 19th-century Romanesque and Queen

Anne styles (that) mix with later Colonial and Classical Revival buildings on Essex Street, one block removed from the Common," according to the 1986 MHC Reconnaissance Survey Town Report of Lawrence.

Stundzia points out that a "gem of nineteenth-century buildings" and an "everything is right there" vision of this historic area features Unitarian and Baptist churches, a Masonic building, a public library, a grammar school, Lawrence City Hall, and a court house, for starters. "It's a microcosm of the urbanization of a city," says Stundzia.

That urbanization has benefitted and hurt Lawrence, at the same time through the years. Many unfairly peg Lawrence as a down-and-out gritty city with many serious social issues, but in reality, this former textile giant is on the rebound with high-tech and other twenty-first-century businesses taking up shop—courtesy of an ambitious economic development office. There's still a long way to go, but the city has good bones, and that strength can be seen in full glory at the exceptionally well-maintained and often-upgraded Lawrence Common. This wonderful park just goes to show that with a proper vision at the onset, many positive aspects of an industrial city can last forever.

# LEOMINSTER

Known as the "Plastics City" because of its long-standing industry, Leominster is anything but plastic.

Fine neighborhoods, many with commanding hilltop views of hill and mountain ranges, mix with close-knit working class neighborhoods to form a city that feels authentic, substantial, and solid. Although industry, a large shopping mall, strip malls, and many service-oriented businesses in newer buildings have taken away from some of the historical preservation, we are reminded of this central Massachusetts small city's grand history in the Monument Square Historic District. Bound by Main and Water Streets and Grove Avenue, the attractive, well-defined town green takes on a few different names: Leominster Square or The Common. Whatever the name preference, this downtown land is like a living outdoor museum of local history. In 1743 the town common became the First Church meetinghouse site, as an active church congregation was required for any community to gain Massachusetts charter status. The First Church's affiliation was actually Puritan, but then became Unitarian in the early nineteenth century. This caused Calvinist members to leave the building and start what is currently the Pilgrim Congregational Church, also located on the common, according to Mark Bodanza in his January 23, 2009, article, "First Church has rich history" in the *Leominster Champion* newspaper.

Dedication sites dot the town green today, including a Native American mortar, several Veterans memorials, a firefighter's memorial, and a monument in honor of Leominster's second meetinghouse.

Area nineteenth-century buildings, city hall, several churches, and a good number of thriving local businesses help make today's

**The Leominster town green gets colorful in the fall.**

version of downtown Leominster look both modern and historical with no stark contrasts—everything seems to blend well together. A designee on the National Register of Historic Places in 1982, this impressive area of Leominster certainly deserves the accolades as some other small cities in Massachusetts have seen social and financial decline—thus, impeding the past and present of these once attractive communities. Not Leominster!

One of Leominster's great annual events is the Winter Stroll and Mayor's Tree Lighting Ceremony, usually held on a weekend day in early December. The event starts with a parade, music performances, hayrides, trackless train rides, cookie decorating, visit with Santa, and more, according to the City of Leominster website at http://leominsterevents.com/event/winter-stroll-and-mayors-tree-lighting-ceremony/. The tree lighting then follows all the afternoon activities.

Saving the most interesting anecdote for last: Leominster is the birthplace of Johnny Appleseed! Celebrating its beloved resident (real name, John Chapman, who became Johnny Appleseed, and contrary to popular belief, planted nurseries rather than orchards everywhere he went). Leominster hosts the Johnny Appleseed Festival on the town common every September. The one-day event features entertainment, arts and crafts, an international food court, a chili cook-off, a petting zoo, and moonwalks. More information on this special event can be found at http://leominsterevents.com/event/johnny-appleseed-festival/. Additionally, as a toast to the legendary Leominster resident, the Johnny Appleseed Craft Beer Festival takes place on the town green and West Street, typically on a Saturday in August. For more information log onto www.johnnyappleseedbeerfest.com/.

# LEXINGTON

George Washington wrote in his diary, "the first blood was spilt in the dispute with Great Britain," on the morning in April 19, 1775. In the first conflict seventy-seven Minutemen battled British Regulars; eight Minutemen lost their lives and ten were wounded. Minutemen wounded two British soldiers. After the battle, Samuel Adams exclaimed to John Hancock, "What a glorious morning for America!"

Today the Lexington town green area serves as not only a significant historical reference of the birthplace of America but also as part of a vibrant downtown with its predominantly locally owned and operated shops and restaurants that run a few blocks. The town green and center provide wonderful leisurely walking opportunities with a laid-back, friendly feel that belies its bloody Revolutionary War origins. The Minuteman Bike Trail also runs through downtown Lexington, spanning eleven miles from Cambridge to the east to bordering Bedford to the west. It is considered by many to be the premier bike trail in the Boston suburbs, with a mix of woods, open space, and proximity to Massachusetts Avenue with shopping and restaurants within the bike trail towns and cities.

The town green area includes the famous *Lexington Minuteman* statue (pictured), a Henry H. Kitson creation that was erected in 1900 as a memorial to the Lexington Minutemen. The town green also features the Revolutionary Monument—the oldest war memorial in the country—completed in 1799. West of the Lexington Battle Green are the gravestones on the Old Burying Ground, dating back to 1690. Some notables buried here include Captain John Parker of the Minutemen and the British soldier wounded on the British retreat

The famous *Lexington Minuteman* graces the central district.

from Concord on April 19, 1775 (who died three days later, at the Buckman Tavern), according to the Tour Lexington website at www .libertyride.us/index.html.

Across the street from the Lexington Battle Green is the Buckman Tavern at 1 Bedford Street. It is the oldest tavern in Lexington and historically significant as the place where about seventy-seven Minutemen gathered in the early hours of April 19, 1775, while awaiting the British Regulars.

The town of Lexington website states, "The tavern was licensed to serve drovers in 1713, and served as a place for churchgoers during the Sunday nooning. The interior today is much the same as it was when the tavern was the headquarters of the Minutemen. Among the many items on display is the Tavern's old front door with a bullet hole from the 1775 Battle of Lexington. To the left of the tavern is the Memorial to the Lexington Minutemen of 1775, erected in 1949, and containing the names of the Minutemen who died on the Green in the first battle of the Revolutionary War." The inscription reads: THESE MEN GAVE EVERYTHING DEAR IN LIFE YEA AND LIFE ITSELF IN SUPPORT OF THE COMMON CAUSE.

The Lexington town green area is home to the Lexington Visitors Center at 1875 Massachusetts Avenue (781-862-1450). The center is open 362 days a year, and the folks here are extremely knowledgeable and passionate about Lexington history. The center features a diorama of the Battle of Lexington, a gift shop, and restrooms.

Adjacent to the visitor center is the USS *Lexington* Memorial dedicated to the memory of those serving aboard the ships that have been named *Lexington*. The USS *Lexington* ship's bell is on display at the Lexington Visitors Center.

For those seeking a big green lawn with plenty of shade, you'd be hard-pressed to find a more attractive town common—or historical one, for that matter. April brings one of the biggest events in the state to the town green where thousands turn out to witness the Battle of Lexington reenactment as part of Patriots Day Weekend festivities in the Lexington-Concord area.

# LONGMEADOW

This Springfield suburb features a spectacular three-quarters-of-a-mile-long town green that looks, interestingly enough, like a long meadow. Not just any long meadow, mind you, as flawless landscaping with freshly cut grass and plantings combine with what seems like perfectly formed trees to create this idyllic setting that clearly reflects an upscale town filled with pride and natural beauty.

Clearly one of the most attractive suburbs in Massachusetts, this quaint New England town owes much of its personality to the town green area. As part of the Longmeadow Historic District, as well as being listed on the National Register of Historic Places in 1982, the Longmeadow town green—bounded by US 5 on the west side and a quaint residential road on the east—dates back to the early eighteenth century, and after many uses it became a park in the late nineteenth century. The Longmeadow town green also holds the rare Massachusetts town common distinction of originating as a sand drift before long-term community nurturing of the space started in 1703.

As the eternal pulse of the community, the town green area featured the first meetinghouse in 1716 and several "cottage industries" in the nineteenth century. In 1898, however, all structures were eliminated on the green and it was returned to its original undeveloped state as the Village Green. That town green now showcases a wonderful concentration of trees and grass and no "overmemorialization." The only structure remaining on the town green is the War Memorial.

The Longmeadow Historic District features some of the best-preserved historic buildings from the eighteenth and nineteenth centuries in the six-state New England region. Those structures majestically

**The Longmeadow town common spans three quarters of a mile.**

surround the village green with a few important twentieth-century additions, like the Town Hall (1930), the Storrs Public Library (built in a charming brick Colonial Revival style from 1932), and the original Center School building (1928). Other standout structures include the First Congregational Church (1768) and the Old Country Store (1805), which is now a spa. More than forty homes from 1725 to 1910 lend incredible and diverse personality to the village green area and the Longmeadow Historic District in general. The Great Places in Massachusetts Commission named the district as one of one thousand great destinations to visit in Massachusetts.

# MANSFIELD

Call the Mansfield town common the Rodney Dangerfield of Massachusetts town greens. Outside of its own town, it gets no respect.

Virtually all town greens in this book have been personally recommended to this writer and many appear prolifically in various publications and on websites. Not Mansfield, first settled in 1658 and officially incorporated in 1775.

Too bad, as the Mansfield South Common, as it is formally called, is one of the more impressive town greens in Massachusetts. Perhaps this lack of notice coincides with Mansfield's own history. Other than public sentiment against slavery escalating in 1836 during the Anti-Slavery Riot of 1836 and Mansfield's men protecting our freedoms in the French and Indian War, the War of 1812, the Civil War, and contemporary history wars, Mansfield has experienced a relatively quiet existence within its own geographical confines. In a state like Massachusetts, home to the Revolutionary War and where freedom of speech often takes on a loud and clear stance (from Thoreau to Harvard-area Vietnam protests of the 1960s to Senator Elizabeth Warren railing out against the big banks), Mansfield often goes about its business without a lot of controversy. This could be due, in part, to its humble, working-class origins steeped in the jewelry, soap, cotton, gristmill, and iron industries.

The town green reflects that working-class aura where families stroll the area after a hard day's work, and the Town Selectmen are very protective of the green's purity. In September 2015, Selectmen declined to allow signs for "Mansfield Bank's Bootcamp for Women" exercise event, according to a September 10, 2015, article in the *Sun Chronicle*.

**A sign that shows the distances to all Mansfields in the world sits at the foot of the town green.**

"It sets up a precedent," Selectmen Chairman George Dentino said after the meeting.

The Mansfield town common looks like many others, with a gazebo, paved walkway, neat landscaping, and historic monuments, but it also possesses unique elements. The unusual copper steel steeple at the top of the mid-nineteenth-century Mansfield Congregational Church on West Street surely catches the eye. At the foot of the town green off Main Street is a post with signs signifying other Mansfields around the world and the distances to those towns from the Massachusetts town with that name. Mansfield, Germany is the farthest away at 3,786 miles! Right behind the gazebo is a structure that looks like a church with its stone facade and a long stained-glass window on the second floor, but it's actually headquarters for the Mansfield School Department—and before that, a public library. The real showstopper, however, occurs in May with the Field of Honor, where 250 flags fly over South Common in honor of local veterans. 🍂

# NATICK

Natick, a western Boston suburb, has seen incredible commercial and residential growth since the 1950s—particularly the wall of retail stores that align with Route 9—but you'd never know it by strolling the town green. Located in an established downtown that looks and feels quaint (save the commuting traffic), the Natick town common has roots that go back to 1841, when local resident Ruel Morse acquired the land for twenty-five thousand dollars with the hopes of a Town Hall being built on the property. While that never happened,

**History surrounds the Natick town common.**

the town green evolved into a downtown park with a Civil War monument erected in 1866, and the wooden gazebo in 1985. Today the Saturday Farmers' Market is a favorite during the summer, as well as the Summer Concert Series on Monday night. Given the attractiveness of the Natick town green, the annual tree-lighting ceremony in late November or early December is quite popular, as the community comes together to trim and light the tree, enjoy holiday characters including Santa, and some hot chocolate.

# NEW SALEM

Very few town centers are located on a dead-end road, but that's the case with New Salem. The lack of a through road, however, works to the tremendous advantage of lovers of the quieter side of New England, as the central district lacks traffic; suburban and urban noise; and commercial, residential, and industrial development. All that's left to enjoy is a lovely town common surrounded by old homes and buildings. Adding another layer to a town protected by the lack of a town center roadway is that the construction of the Quabbin Reservoir in the 1930s has kept much of the land in New Salem inaccessible, as the Metropolitan District Commission controls much of the area near the Quabbin.

This central district is not just about peace and solitude, however. History has been kept so well intact that the National Register of Historic Places designated New Salem in 1978 on its National Register of Historic Places. The town common area features thirty-five buildings, artifacts, and sites, with most of the buildings dating back to the nineteenth century, according to the "National Register of Historic Places nomination for New Salem Center Historic District" application. The town green first appeared in 1734 when its first town leaders set aside a grant to create the parcel that would, through the years, be used as a "training ground for soldiers of the Revolution and War of 1812, the common, a pound, churches, houses, tannery, shops, schools and taverns," according to the Waymarking.com New Salem web page (www .waymarking.com/waymarks/WMHN0G_New_Salem_Common_ Historic_District_New_Salem_MA).

**The New Salem town common lends a peaceful, rural presence.**

New Salem's pride-and-joy event is the Old Home Day that takes place on a Saturday, usually the third week in July. Traditional events, according to the Town of New Salem Old Home Day website, include the following:

- Firemen's Breakfast
- Congregational Church Lunch
- Firemen's Lunch
- Vendors
- 1794 Meetinghouse Silent Auction
- Council on Aging Tin Can Auction
- Parade
- Sporting contests
- Library Book Sale
- Arts & Crafts Show
- Free pony rides
- A bounce house
- An evening presentation by the 1794 Meetinghouse

Finally, an interesting fact: New Salem was named for the settlers from Salem that founded the town.

# NORFOLK

Is it possible for a Boston suburb to be semirural and be located away from all highways? In the case of Norfolk, the answer is yes, and this will probably always be the case due to its strict zoning and development laws. Perhaps the best way to get a true taste of this friendly little southwest of Boston town is by visiting the Norfolk town common. It's a real beauty located above stone walls surrounded from the stately Federated Church, Norfolk Public Library, and Norfolk Town

**The Norfolk town common looks so inviting with its large parcel of green grass.**

Hall. Nicely updated with a gazebo and nicely landscaped lawn, the Norfolk town common is not easily found while driving through the central district. Only by driving off the main route and parking near the Norfolk Public Library can a visitor truly get the full impact of this beautiful town common. All of a sudden—seemingly out of nowhere—this great expanse of land becomes fully juxtaposed with a quaint town center church to create a scene that looks more like Vermont than Massachusetts.

The pretty town common surely reflects the presence of a semirural town located on an upper valley of the Charles River (yes, the same one that everyone knows in Boston and Cambridge). Norfolk became an independent town in 1870 after breaking away from neighboring Wrentham—this after being abandoned during King Philips War and later becoming an agricultural, lumber, and cotton-manufacturing town before becoming established as a residential community with homes and farms.

Because of Norfolk's small-town persona and lack of development, many residents use the town common as a central gathering place for events like a tree-lighting ceremony and Santa parade in December and a concert series each Thursday in summer.

# NORTH ANDOVER

North Andover has it all backward when it comes to significantly historic Massachusetts town greens.

The area now known as North Andover did have a town common, but the land was then part of Andover when in 1634 the Massachusetts General Court set aside sections south of the Merrimack River around Lake Cochichewick and the Shawsheen River for the purpose of creating an inland plantation. In the early years, the spread of settlement south and west of the old town center created much conflict about the location of the parish church. The Massachusetts General Court designated two parish churches, north and south. On April 7, 1855, the north parish then split from the south, thus leading to the incorporation of North Andover.

After the American Revolution, North Andover—like so many other towns—looked to build a small town and bought swampland to set aside as the town common, according to Carol J. Majahad, executive director of the North Andover Historical Society. The location proved to be ideal with, today, the presence of a town with businesses and old homes surrounding the town green. But old problems never go away, and the current-day town common is prone to flooding due to its swamp origins.

The Village Improvement Society owned the land from 1886 to 1959, when, at that point, North Andover gave it to the town.

**The North Andover town common leads to the historic North Parish Church.**

During its association with the Village Improvement Society, North Andover became "old" again with a dedication to creating a "Colonial Revival" look, according to Majahad. So, the combination of historic preservation and town green renovations make an innately historic four-acre town green look even more historic. The most prominent structure is the North Parish Church, which dates back to 1836—the fifth meetinghouse of the Puritan church congregation founded in 1645 in North Andover. The congregation became a Unitarian church in 1836. Additionally, several pre-1720 homes still exist in the area.

"The town common used to be a crossroads to other towns," says Majahad. "So, the nineteenth-century village never went anywhere. It looks today what it looked like one hundred years ago."

The town green isn't saturated with monuments, stones, and markers like many other Massachusetts town commons, but what exists resonates with uniqueness. A statue of Phillips Brooks honors the local who was not only a great-grandson of Samuel Phillips Jr., founder of Phillips Academy Andover, but most prominently an American Episcopal clergyman and author, a rector of Boston's Trinity Church, briefly a bishop of Massachusetts, and the lyricist of the Christmas hymn, "O Little Town of Bethlehem."

In 1959 North Andover planted exotic trees and pathways, but the left of the town common shows no path. What is there is rusticated seating, or put more simply, stone walls to sit and take in the presence of the attractive North Andover town green, says Majahad.

The North Andover town green holds many seasonal events; the most notable is the traditional Sheep Sheering that dates back to the 1960s. It is traditionally held the third Sunday in May. There's also a Fourth of July celebration, fall festival held the last Saturday in September, and Sunday evening summer concerts on the common.

# NORWOOD

Locals love to frequent the Norwood Town Common. Why? Well, it all centers on town pride, and as they say, "Once you live in Norwood, you never move out." That means getting to love the town and discovering all that it has to offer.

Unlike many other Massachusetts town greens, the creation of Norwood's town common did not coincide with the incorporation of the town in 1872. According to a town historian, Patricia Fanning, the area remained a group of older structures and buildings for quite some time. A new town common and center gradually took shape around 1912 (when it was first envisioned by George Willett, who was chairman of the Town Planning Board) until the erection of the current Municipal Building, which was dedicated in 1928.

Astonishingly, the historic-looking Norwood town common/ square is not part of any designated local, state, or federal historic district. Created in the 1920s (first envisioned by Willett) with the erection of the Norwood Memorial Municipal Building (town hall) in memory of World War I veterans, it was renamed the Veterans of Foreign Wars Park following World War II.

According to Fanning, the "Protectors of the American Way" monument, which stands at the corner of Nahatan and Washington Streets, was created by sculptor Robert Shure of Woburn, Massachusetts. This tribute was made possible by longtime Norwood resident and businessman Frank Simoni. A veteran of two wars, Simoni was impressed by the remarkable monuments he saw while visiting Europe. In 1988 he decided he wanted to memorialize, on a grand scale, "those who sacrificed their lives to protect freedom." The final product—three

**A bandstand with the historic Norwood Theater in the background gives Norwood a classic "Main Street USA" feel.**

nine-foot figures of a father, mother, and child—represents the American family. It is guarded on three sides by bronzed military personnel representing the nation's armed forces, says Fanning.

A short distance from this monument stands a memorial stone dedicated to the men and women from Norwood who received the US Army Combat Infantry Badge.

Fanning adds that the Walter J. Dempsey Memorial Bandstand, which stands at the center of the common, was dedicated in 1993 as a lasting memorial to a well-respected local businessman and long-term selectman. Concerts are held in the bandstand every summer (usually on Wednesday and Sunday evenings). Couples use the bandstand both for wedding ceremonies and photos.

Various groups use the common for other purposes with the Board of Selectmen's approval. For example, the Circle of Hope, a local charitable organization that aids Norwood residents in need, uses the common for an Illumination Night each December as a fundraiser. It is also the site of the local farmers' market, holiday tree lighting and storytelling in November, and other events.

In a little more than one hundred years, the Norwood town common has evolved to look like older, more historic Massachusetts town greens. Six paths lead from the gazebo, with four leading to the corners and two from the midpoints. The town common itself is rather typical with no outstanding characteristics, but the surrounding area makes it quite special. The old St. Catherine's Church and United Church of Norwood majestically rise from the Washington Street side of the downtown, while the renovated old-time Norwood Theater—with its classic marquee—graces the Central Street side. A walk to Washington Street reveals an excellent mix of American and ethnic restaurants—the latter including Middle Eastern, Asian, Italian, Thai, and Southwestern cuisines.

Norwood used to be part of Dedham, but after years of locals "pestering" town officials about the need for its own parish and the horrible road conditions, Norwood became a community of its own. Transitioning from an agricultural community to an industrial one, Norwood today has many urban elements within its small-town setting, but the town green stays true to form as an open oasis—one of the few remaining in densely populated, built-up Massachusetts towns.

# PETERSHAM

This small north-central Massachusetts town—located on a high ridge that makes it prone to beautiful sunrises and sunsets—has what is generally regarded as one of the most classic town greens in New England. It is like a greatest-hits collection of town greens with number-one hits like a gazebo, beautiful open space, and, just off the land, churches, an old public library, amazing Gothic revival homes, and a wonderful country store dating back to 1843 that has been beautifully restored. The town green is located in the Petersham Historic District, containing more than forty structures from the mid-1700s to the mid-1900s and is home to fine examples of a wide range of architectural styles including Colonial, Greek Revival, Federal, Shingle-style, and Contemporary. The whole scene looks stunning, but it would be nothing if not for the close-knit community that utilizes this green space as a place to gather as neighbors and friends.

"I am a (Petersham) native," says Ari Pugliese, owner of The Country Store in Petersham (more on this historic business in a moment). "I have always been inspired by central places to gather. You see that all over Europe. Sense of isolation is a big problem in our society. For me, most impressive is not just the physical beauty of the (Petersham) town common but a place to congregate. It's a great place to gather."

When asked about favorite town commons in Massachusetts, Paul Danahy—a former Barre resident who lives most of the year in Florida—does not hesitate to say, "Petersham! (It is) surrounded by stately homes and buildings not to mention that great country store!"

**Many consider the Petersham town green the prototype for a traditional New England town common.**

The town common is put to good use with the Petersham Farmers' Market every Friday during the summer, the Old Home Day town day in August, and summer concerts on the common.

Petersham was incorporated in 1754 and is known for being the second battle site for Shaw's Rebellion, an uprising by Massachusetts citizens against the state for levying additional taxes to pay for debt problems. Located at the northern end of the Quabbin Reservoir, Petersham possesses most of the elements that comprise a classic New England village—that is, with most of the residents living near the center, an emphasis on preservation and incredible absence of modern development and a surplus of fertile farmland on the outskirts.

Right off the town green is Petersham's version of an anchor store: The Country Store in Petersham. The Country Store in Petersham might not be one of those country stores that offers everything under the sun, but it does radiate an authenticity and welcoming nature that few other stores of its kind can match.

The location certainly helps—right across from one of New England's most beautiful town commons—but this north-central

Massachusetts country store stands quite nicely on its own, with a grocery store featuring foods mostly made or sourced locally, baked goods and frozen treats, a restaurant, Vermont cheese, and a modest selection of nice gifts.

Discovering this local treasure with the exterior Greek Revival architecture and interior classic country store appearance surely satiates the quest for a classic New England county store travel experience, but what makes it even more heartwarming is what has happened over the past few years. After serving the community since 1843, The Petersham Country Store sadly closed in 2012. A strong community resolve, however, stopped this landmark from becoming a faded memory, as the East Quabbin Land Trust purchased the building in 2013 and reopened it in 2014 under the management of Ari and Jeanneane Pugliese. The Country Store in Petersham has come back to life mightily with a steady customer base, a clear pride of ownership, and an innate spirit that not only originates from its storied history but through a community that holds tradition and local businesses in the highest regard. Together with the adjacent town green, the combination makes for one of the most authentic traditional village scenes in Massachusetts.

Petersham is especially beautiful in the fall when the colorful leaves, crisp chill in the air, and the plentiful apple-picking farms in the area make for a truly memorable small-town experience. Locals know this to be true, but the mainstream travel media have also picked up on rural Petersham's virtues. *Travel + Leisure* in its "Best Affordable Fall Foliage Towns" states, "The Berkshires may be more famous than the rolling hills of Central Massachusetts, but this sleepy area offers timeless towns like Petersham. Just 90 minutes from Boston, Petersham offers a classic New England town green, white clapboard houses, and century-old maple trees, while the surrounding dense forest explodes into reds, oranges, and yellows come late September."

# PITTSFIELD

Park Square, a 1.5-acre oval green in the heart of downtown Pittsfield, exhibits a remarkable concentration of civic, religious, and commercial structures dating back to the early nineteenth century. Located at the highest point of Pittsfield within the Berkshires Mountains of western Massachusetts region, this spot has seen a meetinghouse first built in 1762, land donated for a town common in 1790, a beautification project by Pittsfield residents in 1824, and a second round of improvements in 1871 and 1872, according to the Cultural Landscape Foundation web page (https://tclf.org/landscapes/pittsfield -park-square). At that time, the green's oval plot improved with a broad gravel walk with granite curbing, site grading, and a replanting of two rows of trees. The revitalization happens with frequency to this very day, a clear sign of city pride.

This square has several interesting historic anecdotes. For example, a giant white elm tree, located in the town green's center, fell in 1861, after 340 years of existence. Also, the nation's first agricultural fair happened here in August 1810, according to the National Register of Historic Places Inventory for Pittsfield. Additionally, and more significantly, soldiers mustered at Park Square to fight in the American Revolution, the War of 1812, and the Civil War.

Following through with ongoing upgrades, the Berkshire Group renovated the park in the 1990s, as the Culture Landscape Society describes so well: "a concrete sidewalk lines the perimeter and transects the oval space in two axes, creating quadrants of lawn, meeting at a large historic fountain at the center of the park. The park also features historic site furnishings and seasonal flower beds." A Civil War me-

**Distant mountain views and a vibrant downtown provide a nice setting for Pittsfield's Park Square—and vice versa.**

morial from 1872 stands as perhaps the most significant structure in the park.

The Pittsfield Park Square Historic District encompasses many city blocks adjacent to Park Square at the junction of North, South, East, and West Streets. Structures facing south of the park, according to the National Register of Historic Places Nomination Form for Pittsfield, include the Berkshire County Savings Bank building (1894–1896), the Gothic Revival Congregational Church (1853), and the Old Town Hall (1832). The English Gothic Revival St. Stephen's Church cornerstone was laid in 1889 and the edifice consecrated by the Right Reverend Phillips Brooks in 1892. Facing north of the park is the Lombardi Romanesque Berkshire County Courthouse (1872) and the Venetian Gothic Berkshire Athenaeum (1876).

Although General Electric's departure from Pittsfield in the late 1980s caused significant economic depression, locals never gave up, and today the downtown has experienced an impressive renaissance with a growing cultural, dining, and retail scene. At the very center of this revitalization is an entity that never really went away—that is, Park Square. The green's events include summer concerts, December Christmas festivities, parts of the July Ethnic Fair and Fourth of July parade, free zumba, the Field of Flags in November to honor veterans, and many Third Thursday street festival events.

Add that impressive concentration of buildings—many still used one hundred–plus years later—and the Park Square and Historic District clearly stands as one of the most impressive, vibrant, significantly historic urban areas of the state.

# PLYMOUTH

Most people know of Plymouth as the Pilgrim's landing destination in 1620, having set sail from England on the *Mayflower* with many in search of religious freedom. While the Pilgrims dominate Plymouth history, it's a good idea to take a pilgrimage into other aspects of its culture—like the Plymouth Training Green, first appearing on town records in 1711. That makes this town green one of the oldest in the country! For more than three hundred years, this green space has been used for "training militia to grazing cattle, from temperance lectures to art shows," as stated by Karin Goldstein in her superb article "The Training Green: From Training to Temperance to Art" that appeared in the October 2, 2011, edition of the *Plymouth Patch* (website page address: http://patch.com/massachusetts/plymouth/the-training -green-from-traning-to-temperance-to-art).

The Training Green is located on Sandwich Street in Downtown Plymouth, just south of the Town Square, and became a memorial park in 1889—neatly designed to more of a parklike presence, including curvilinear paths, by the famous Olmsted landscaping firm. The most prominent attraction is the Soldiers and Sailors Monument, dedicated in 1869 and built of granite—with the names of troops killed in the Civil War inscribed in the stone. The last time soldiers trained here was during World War II, according to a May 27, 2011, article in the *Plymouth Patch* (http://patch.com/massachusetts/plymouth/ remembering-the-training-green-on-memorial-day).

Goldstein also writes about a gun house built on the premises: "In 1820, the town permitted the state to construct a gun house on the northeast corner of the Training Green for use by the Plymouth

**An American flag flies proudly at Plymouth's Training Green.**

Artillery Company, founded in 1777. The building stood about thirty years—around 1850, the gun house was purchased by Henry Whiting, Jr., for a residence, and moved to Sandwich St. near Winter St."

She adds that the Town of Plymouth "invested in fire engines in the 1830s, and constructed a building to house the suction-engine fountain in 1831 on the southwest side of the Green." A reservoir to supply the engine was added three years later, "but the firehouse was dismantled when steam-powered fire engines replaced the old suction engines."

Cows grazed on the Training Green in the nineteenth century, and people peacefully coincided with the cattle for lectures and public gatherings.

Today, the Training Green remains true to form with the Training Monument intact, the Olmsted walkways still looking good, and the park put to good use, with people walking the peaceful environs, the Plymouth Guild Art Show putting on shows, and the town doing a fine job of maintaining the integrity of the land.

# PRINCETON

The Princeton town common is a beauty—a large expanse of hilltop land with a gazebo and, just off the green, a majestic town hall, a public library built in 1883, and the Congregational Church (the former third meetinghouse) constructed in 1838. With that advantageous location, one can see on a clear day all the way to Boston (about forty-five miles away). It's the perfect town common in which to unwind, reflect, and get in the traditional New England spirit.

After the separation of church and state, the Congregational Church was moved from the head of the common to its present site, thus leaving the town common with no major structures until the construction of a gazebo in the 1990s, according to local historian Nancy Orlando.

Princeton, established in 1759 and incorporated in 1771, once supported its own company of Minutemen during the Colonial days, thrived as an agricultural town (Boston's famous Parker House once featured "Blueberries from Princeton" on its menu), and then showcased industries specializing in hat making, lumbering, and chair making, states G. H. Beaman in "A Brief History of Princeton" (www .town.princeton.ma.us/Pages/PrincetonMA_WebDocs/brief). What separates Princeton from many other Massachusetts towns steeped in agricultural and industrial endeavors, however, is that this picturesque country town served as a vacation destination during the late 1800s and early 1900s, with eight trains a day bringing hundreds of visitors to hotels and boarding houses. Some famous visitors signed hotel registers: Louisa May Alcott, Sarah Bernhardt, Lydia Pinkham, the Harpers of *Harper's* magazine, and Thomas Edison, according to Beaman.

**A bandstand, town hall, and historic church lend a beautiful look to the Princeton town green.**

With the advent of the automobile, however, vacation preferences changed and Princeton reverted back to a quiet little village (with the exception of Mount Wachusett, a prominent ski destination located on the northern side of town).

Walking the town common today, one can sense the rest-and-relaxation vibe that once made this former predominantly agricultural and lumber town an appealing vacation destination. From the hilly town green, pleasing panoramic views of the hills and mountains in the distance and older homes surrounding the green evoke a true rural feeling that belies its proximity to Fitchburg, Leominster, and Worcester—the latter being the second-most populated city in New England.

# PROVINCETOWN

The Provincetown town green—also known as the Bas Relief—demonstrates a true work of progress in one of Cape Cod's most interesting and appealing vacation destinations. Not as old as many of the other town greens in Massachusetts, Provincetown's version began in 1922 as an Olmsted-designed space to provide a green oasis in an otherwise sandy, exposed seaside village, as described in the Massachusetts Department of Conservation's (DCR) "Common Wealth: The Past and Future of Town Commons." Certainly not a bad way to enter the field of Massachusetts town commons—that is, being designed by a famous landscaper—the Provincetown town green, unfortunately, became a bit frayed due to neglect and the punishing elements of the sea. By the early 2000s, the green approached blighted status as "the walks had cracked, creating hazards for pedestrians, and the trees had matured and multiplied, obscuring the sculpture and shading the lawn," according to the DCR's report.

Provincetown turned an increasingly bad situation around quickly by following the Americans with Disabilities Act Accessibility Guideline to provide safe walkways—long-lasting brick pavers replaced the concrete and adhered to "stable, firm and slip-resistant" requirements. Then, Cape crusaders (sorry for the bad pun) took the integrity of the Provincetown Bas Relief to the next level. They made the landscape more visible by removing some trees and "planted small trees, perennials and shrubs along the walks' outside edges, adding color and texture to the green," according to the DCR.

The final touch: Taking the *Field of Dreams* "Build it and they will come" theory and marketing the town green as a vital part of the

**The Pilgrim Monument towers above the Provincetown town green.**

Provincetown experience with public events. Those events include a Portuguese Festival held in late June, a Women's Week in mid-October, and a Family Week in late July. For a full list of events at the town green, log onto the Provincetown Chamber of Commerce's website at http://ptownchamber.com/, or visit them at 307 Commercial Street in Lopes Square (508-487-3424).

Virtually just a few steps off the town green is the Pilgrim Monument, built between 1907 and 1910, to commemorate the first landing of the *Mayflower* Pilgrims in Provincetown on November 21, 1620. Yes, that's correct—Provincetown was the Pilgrim's first landing in the United States, not Plymouth. President Theodore Roosevelt laid the cornerstone on August 20, 1907, and President William H. Taft led the dedication ceremony after the Pilgrim Monument's completion. The tower is 252 feet, 7.5 inches tall and rises 350 feet above sea level, making it the tallest all-granite structure in the United States! For those looking for a nice walk, the trip to the top of the monument takes about ten minutes with 116 steps and 60 ramps along the way.

While it might seems out of place to mention a town green that has not yet reached its one hundredth anniversary, Provincetown's ambition to potentiate an Olmsted-designed common to a current-day gem is one of historic proportions. With so much to see and do in Provincetown—with its unique shops, vibrant dining scenes, cultural opportunities, and beach life—the town green more than holds its own as a major Provincetown destination.

# ROWLEY

Salem, Rockport, Gloucester, and Marblehead get most of the attention when it comes to travel destinations in the North Shore area of Massachusetts, but many locals often passionately converse about how the smaller, lesser-known towns are nicest. Rowley repeatedly comes up in those conversations.

Not a tourist destination by any means, Rowley, instead, stands out as an unassuming pretty community that prides itself on small-town life and historic preservation. The streets are filled with beautiful Colonial homes from various eras, but it is the town common district that truly brings together the personality of the town. Also known as the Training Place (this is where Benedict Arnold's expedition to Quebec encamped in 1775 during the American Revolution), the Rowley town common today features a Civil War Memorial, a bandstand, a baseball field, and many town events. July through September features the Rowley Farmers' Market on Sunday morning at the town green.

Rowley is one of those "you-had-to-be-there" type of towns. There's no way to fully capture the magic of the town in writing. Rather the town can only be fully appreciated by being there. An unidentified writer, however, states it so accurately:

> It is one of the pleasantest towns in Essex County. There is everything about it substantial, prosperous and agreeable. In the summer season, it is hardly possible to go over the green hillocks, and through the quiet intervals, along the roads, dust laid by the late showers, or by the sparkling brooks fringed with luxuriant grass and flowers, and see the quiet and peace reigning

**A Civil War memorial stands out at the Rowley town common.**

everywhere in this old town,—the contentment and prosperity of its stable farmers, and the thrift and joyousness of its active mechanics, without wishing that we had been born in Rowley; that it had been our lot first to have heard there the lowing of the cattle, and down its hillsides to have tumbled the ripened pumpkins, when autumn yellowed the leaves. Let the world go. To be born in such a place, and in the sereneness of old age to die in such a place, and to sleep at last in the same dust with the good old fathers of olden times, were enough to fill the cup of mortal happiness full.

That special place in Rowley could start in any location, but the town green always stands as an optimal place to begin this small town exploration.

# ROYALSTON

Royalston proves that the best change is no change at all.

This tiny north-central Massachusetts town, not too far from the Quabbin Reservoir, is all about preservation—largely seen in the Royalston Common Historic District. When the Village Improvements and Historical Society of Royalston was founded in 1946, the first assignment was to save Schoolhouse #1, and they succeeded. The building serves as a museum and post office.

According to the Historical Society, "Recent projects include restoring the ornate fence surrounding 'The Bastille' which is mostly on public land and the acquisition of a collection of 18th century papers from early town settlers."

Thankfully, the town common has been wonderfully preserved, so the scene looks quite similar to when the town named after Isaac Royal, a slaveholder and businessperson from Medford, founded the town in a land deal in 1765. Through the years, Royalston would possess all the earmarks of a classic New England town, with its town common, town hall, church, public library, and post office (the latter located in the Royalston Historical Society) all set around the common and the Royalston Common Historic District. The area is so quaint and quiet that many wealthy people frequented the town in the 1920s as a restful getaway.

Other than Royalston no longer being a vacation getaway, not too much has changed around the town common, as the sixteen or so homes—built from 1780 to 1840—are all painted a white color, with the exception of one painted yellow, according to Royalston Historical Society curator John McClure. The homeowner of that house was

**Fall foliage arrives in full glory at the Royalston town green.**

granted permission by the Royalston Historic District to have a yellow house, as a paint chip from when the house was first built revealed that color. McClure says that homes can only possess three colors for shutters—white, green, or blue—and there is only one of the latter. The only thing that has changed on the town common are the trees, as the old elms died, were replaced by maples, and those maples have been supplanted by newer ones. McClure adds that no mailboxes are allowed around the town common, so all residents—who are mostly part of the Royalston Historical Society—have to use post office boxes. But there is no standalone post office, as it is located in the Historical Society building with morning hours only. In the center district, you'll see no gas stations, commercial stores, or signs, just nearly fifty historic homes and buildings. Unspoiled and unchanged is the best way to describe the Royalston Historic District—such a rarity along the industrial-charged Eastern seaboard.

Quirky, fascinating stories have evolved around the town common, too, including a stay by Empress Zita—the last empress of Austria, the last queen of Hungary, and the last queen of Bohemia—who with "seven of her eight children (stayed) for several summers at La Bastille (an 1819 historic home at the common) after they fled their adopted Belgium in 1940 following a Nazi invasion," according to Rob Brinkley's "All Is Calm" article (April 30, 2102) in *New England Home* magazine. The article states that Zita "was the widow of Emperor Karl, the ruler of the Austro-Hungarian Empire from 1916 to his abdication in 1918, who died in 1922 in exile in Portugal." Her connection to Royalston: a friendship with the prominent Bullock family, who owned the house at the time.

Zita and family were "Europe's most distinguished refugees," said an article in *Life* magazine in December 1940.

Royalston celebrated its 250th anniversary on and around the town green in September 2015 with a parade, entertainment, food, and local arts and crafts. A tree-lighting ceremony takes place in front of Town Hall in December—at the town common—and concerts on the common take place at Bullock Field (right in back of the town common).

The town comes in at an astounding 42.5 square miles with some truly beautiful countryside and scenic Tully Lake, but the town center truly offers the best sense of Royalston's historic personality.

# SALEM

Salem might be known as the "Witch City," but there's plenty more brewing in this small city located on the North Shore of Massachusetts.

The nine-acre Salem Common, formally known as Washington Square, dates back to 1714 when it was set aside as a training field for the local population. In the early 1800s, however, the template of Salem Common evolved with gates and a fence and classic neoclassical brick mansions facing the common. Revival-style homes filled out any empty spaces in the early to mid-nineteenth century.

Today Salem Common features a gazebo, a gravel walking path around the town green, and plenty of benches. The wrought-iron fence around Salem Common was built in 1850 but has undergone extensive renovation. Architect Samuel McIntire originally designed the white archway near the northside entrance, but the deteriorating condition of the structure prompted a replica to be constructed in 1976, according to "History of the Salem Common District" on the Salem Common Neighborhood Association website (www.salem common.org/history/).

Several homes around the town green possess historical significance. The Joseph Story House (1811) was the residence of former US Supreme Court Justice Joseph Story. Designated as a National Register of Historic Places home in 1973, the Story House is also a National Historic Landmark. The Andrew-Safford House (1819), originally built for a wealthy Russian fur merchant, is a Federal-style home now owned by the Peabody Essex Museum, according to the Historic Buildings of Massachusetts website (http://mass.historic buildingsct.com/?p=2867).

**Historic brick mansions surround Washington Square.**

Salem is the birthplace of the US Army National Guard, and its origins can be traced back to 1637 at Salem Common, according to "History of the Salem Common Historic District." The first muster took place at the Salem Common when a regiment of militia drilled for the common defense of a multi-community area. This gathering served as a precursor to what would eventually become the National Guard. Former Governor Deval Patrick signed HB1145 in 2010: "An Act Designating the City of Salem as the Birthplace of the National Guard." President Barack Obama on January 10, 2013, signed executive order HR1339, "which designates the City of Salem, Mass., as the birthplace of the U.S. National Guard." A big celebration followed at the Salem Common on April 14, 2012, when Salem celebrated the 375th anniversary of the first muster with more than one thousand soldiers participating in a parade and ceremonies.

With all the rich history, it's no surprise that the Salem Common Historic District—bounded roughly by St. Peter's, Bridge, and Derby Streets and Collins Cove—was added to the National Register of Historic Places in 1976. The history continues virtually throughout all of Salem, particularly the Chestnut Street District. Situated near the town green, the Chestnut Street District features some of the finest examples of grand Federal mansions in the United States, with quite a few designed by Samuel McIntire.

Because Salem Common is just steps away from the wonderful Essex Street pedestrian shopping district and Pickering Wharf—with a collective fabulous mix of museums, stores, restaurants, galleries, and boutiques—the chance to enjoy most of historic Salem requires just a few short pleasant walks from the town green.

# SHIRLEY

What do the father of the Appalachian Trail and the Shirley Common Historic District have in common?

Famous American forester, planner, and conservationist Benton MacKeye (he first had the idea of starting the Appalachian Trail in 1921) had a love for both. MacKeye, also cofounder of the Wilderness Society (1935) and the Regional Planning Association of America (1923), moved frequently as a child, but found true small-town love in Shirley when visiting cousins, according to the "Shirley Center Historic District" article on the National Park Service website (www.nps .gov/nr/travel/massachusetts_conservation/shirley_center.html).

MacKeye once said of the Shirley Center:

> The community par excellence was [and is] the colonial New England village. Take my own hill hamlet—Shirley Center, Massachusetts—as I knew it as a boy, with its seventy-one souls in the 1880s. A meetinghouse, a red brick schoolhouse, a store, farmhouses, wheelwright shop and town hall—seats respectively of religion, education, commerce, agriculture, industry, and government—the basic elements of civilization . . . Except for the motor car and plumbing, this description holds in large measure for Shirley Center today as I sit in my white clapboard house on one of its shaded streets and write these words.

Of course with most great town centers comes an equally great town green, and Shirley surely (sorry for the *Airplane* Leslie Nielsen movie reference) comes through on every level with a classic common.

**The old meetinghouse resides proudly at Shirley's town common.**

The town green, dating back to 1753, is a natural beauty that relies on green grass and Greek Revival, Georgian, and Federal-style architecture homes and buildings, including the town hall from 1848, a meetinghouse dating back to 1773 (clearly no longer a meetinghouse but used for weddings, recitals, concerts, and other functions), a cemetery with its first burial in 1729, and the First Parish Congregational Church. So special is this pure example of a historic district (and with all power lines buried underground to preserve that historical integrity!) and its town green, it was added to the National Register of Historic Places in 1988.

"The Shirley town common is extra special because it is so well maintained—it looks like it did one hundred years ago," says Meredith

Marcinkewicz, curator for the Shirley Historical Society and a long-time Shirley resident.

Monuments include a Civil War plaque at the corner of the cemetery, a Civil War dedication in the middle of the common, and a plaque at the meetinghouse that mentions those who marched off to fight in the Revolutionary War on April 19, 1775.

Current events happening on or around the green include the Shirley Hoedown (Town Day) the first Saturday of June with music, games, food, arts and crafts, and so on; concerts on the common held every other week in the summer on Friday; a farmers' market on Thursday during the summer; and the Holdenwood 10K trail run on the last Saturday of September that starts at the common and benefits town education.

Boy and Girl Scouts hold meetings in the Shirley Town Hall and after their sessions can often be seen "playing games out on the town common," says Marcinkewicz. "It is so nice to see."

Back to Mr. MacKeye. His jobs and passions (often interrelated) took him many places, but he proudly lived in his Shirley Center home until his death in 1975. Marcinkewicz says that a friend of MacKeye gathered all his letters, papers, maps, and other documents and published a book for his friends—and others who wanted to read the book, too. Marcinkewicz says that in the book, MacKeye had a concept on "what makes an old New England village." Those elements are a church, school, general store, home, and town hall.

Thus, Shirley clearly comes through as a true New England village—and one with a town green that serves as a fabulous starting point in this relatively hidden, truly underrated Massachusetts town.

For more information on the Shirley town common and historic district, log onto the Shirley Historical Society and Museum website at www.shirleyhistory.org or call (978) 425-9328.

# SPRINGFIELD

Court Square, in the heart of downtown Springfield, is one of Massachusetts oldest greens dating back to 1636. With the changes in Springfield through the centuries—including serving as a crossroads during the Revolutionary War, being a major Industrial Revolution player, being a victim of urban decline from 1930 to 1970, and experiencing a gradual rebound since then with high-tech, industrial, commercial, and tourism elements—the Court Square common remains one of the only visible constants.

Court Square is bounded by Court Street, Main Street, State Street, East Columbus Avenue, Elm Street, and a wonderful pedestrian-only walkway from the courthouse toward Springfield's historic Old First Church—built in 1819 and listed on the National Register of Historic Places in 1972 (four buildings have been located on the site, with the first constructed in 1645). There's a beautiful gazebo on the premises—built about twenty years ago and featuring a hand-hammered finial standing atop the copper cupola, according to its builder Kleeberg Sheet Metal, Inc.

The Old First Church features a rooster weathervane on the steeple created by a coppersmith in London, England, and brought to this country in 1750, as mentioned on the "Springfield" page of the Revolutionary Day website (www.revolutionaryday.com/usroute20/springfield/default.htm). The Old First Church had some famous churchgoers: inventor Thomas Blanchard and abolitionist John Brown worshipped; Daniel Webster spoke; and Jenny Lind sang, according to the One Financial Plaza "Location" webpage at http://1350mainstreet.com/location/.

**Court Square maintains its historical integrity in an ever-changing downtown.**

The common also features two markers that commemorate the Revolution—a stone and tablet recognizing the site of Parson's Tavern where General George Washington was met on his way to take command of the Continental Army in Boston, according to Wayne Phaneuf's May 29, 2011, article on MassLive.com (www.masslive .com/history/index.ssf/2011/05/springfields_375th_city_monuments _honor_those_who_answered_the_call.html).

As nice as Court Square looks, it could have been a better town green contender, as in 1902 a move was made to extend Court Square to the scenic Connecticut River, but the action was, unfortunately, impeded with the construction of an elevated I-91 and a huge parking

lot beneath it in the late 1950s, according to the I-91 web page (www
.bostonroads.com/roads/I-91_MA/). Still, Court Square, despite its
limitations, serves as a wonderful example of an attractive urban
common—not only for its landscaping and walkways but for what
surrounds the property.

In 1909, famous architect H. H. Richardson designed the Court
House with its gothic stone look (the building now houses the ju-
venile courthouse). The Springfield Municipal Group, erected in
1911–1913, was dedicated by President William Howard Taft in December 1913. President Taft praised the Springfield Municipal Group
in a dedication speech as "one of the most distinctive civic centers in
the United States—and indeed, the world."

The historic district encompassing Court Square and its surrounding buildings became listed on the National Register of Historic
Places in 1974. ⚜

# STERLING

Based on a 1740 deed to the Second Parish of Lancaster, the church, not the town, still owns Sterling's town green. With separation of church and state mostly occurring in the 1820s and 1830s, many of Sterling's selectmen and other town officials were members of the church and didn't feel like any transition was necessary.

Clarence Vernon Gaw, a lifelong Sterling resident and member of the Sterling Historical Society, and with family ties to the famous Sawyer and Butterick families in town, says that when selectmen built a new town hall in 1835, the common remained with the church. "It certainly adds a unique element to town common history," laughs Gaw. "I'm not sure if any towns of Massachusetts still have town common land owned by the church."

Additionally, the road in front of what is now known as the First Church of Sterling (thirty-five Unitarian members own the church, and the church has more than two hundred overall members of various faiths) is also owned by the church. Granted parcels of the land have been transferred to the town through the years, but the main common is well defined and clearly intact.

Gaw says that Sterling pays for the town green's upkeep, and the mutual relationship works well. Unlike in previous years when everything from horses to concerts compromised the green grass, today's look is well landscaped and refined in a casual way.

Sterling, a small north-central Massachusetts town first settled by Europeans in 1720 and officially incorporated in 1781 (after being the Chocksett section of Lancaster), offers, in addition to the attractive town green, a sterling traditional New England look.

**There's no doubt about Sterling's commitment to history with this downtown scene at the town common.**

Compact, cozy, and ultimately charming, the Sterling Center Historic District—bounded by Meetinghouse Hill Road and Main Street, Maple Street and Kendall Hill Road, and Boulding Road, Worcester Road, and Princeton Street—can be admired mostly with a few turns of the head and eyes with good periphery vision.

Best experienced by getting out of the car to truly see the town, walking the town common, by foot, yields a perspective of a much larger area than driving quickly through the central district. Every look from the town common offers a rich slice of history. What a pleasant surprise to find so much history jam-packed into an unassuming district that never seems to get the press that more famous Massachusetts towns and cities hold!

The Sterling town common dominates as the central attraction of this town and has an additionally fascinating history, as it was laid out on three acres in 1724 as a donation by the local Sawyer family. Gaw reports that Elias Sawyer fought in King Philip's War, and with his son became a prisoner taken to Montreal. They were not executed, as their expertise in the sawmill industry (the name Sawyer came from those who worked in the sawmills) proved valuable. The enemy was so pleased with the Sawyers' work that they eventually let the father go home—the son, however, stayed to continue working, says Gaw. Sterling became its own town in 1781 after being part of Lancaster for many years. Lancaster didn't want to let go of the Sterling area, as its apple farms created profit.

The "National Register of Historic Places nomination for the Sterling Center Historic District" application states that at its inception the town common featured a meetinghouse, stables, and two "noon houses" (one for men and one for women). Today the historic district includes many well-maintained eighteenth- and nineteenth-century houses, several church buildings, and the 1835 town hall.

"Once an agricultural town that morphed into cottage industries making hats, needles, clocks, leather goods, shirts, chairs, and pottery, the railway helped matters in the 1850s by opening new markets for agricultural products and manufactured goods," according to a 1991 Sterling Historic District Commission report. Of course history abounds well before this period of time. Sterling could have very well been home to Native Americans as far back as 7,000 BC, states the Historic District report.

To no surprise the district was added to the National Register of Historic Places in 1988. To learn more about this historical gem of a town, the Sterling Historical Society (978-422-6139), at the corner of Maple and Pine Streets, serves as a wonderful resource located in the former MacArthur Estate built around 1760.

Today, agricultural and industrial elements remain, but Sterling today is mostly a residential community. For about one hundred years, the population remained at two thousand, but since 1950 it has grown rapidly to over eight thousand, according to the Town of Sterling website at www.sterling-ma.gov/home/pages/town-history.

# STURBRIDGE

When traveling Route 20 in Sturbridge, many feel that everything they need to know about this pleasant small central Massachusetts town is located on this busy stretch of road. Old Sturbridge Village—an internationally known outdoor living museum attraction that re-creates life in the mid-1800s—and an interesting hodgepodge of restaurants, antiques stores, inns, and locally owned mom-and-pop shops, surely suggest the center of activity in Sturbridge. Unfortunately students and teachers on field trips, vacationers, and even some locals completely bypass the actual town center of Sturbridge, located about two miles east of Old Sturbridge Village on Route 131.

Immediately upon entering the real town center, you know you've arrived in traditional New England—with two historical icons lending the small-town vibe often missing from commercial-laden Route 20. The first is the Publick House—formerly the first public meetinghouse in town—and now a Colonial-style restaurant and inn with a tradition of beautiful tall elm trees first planted in 1791. And the second, of course, is the Sturbridge town common, a destination that looks so familiar—maybe because it embodies the quintessential New England town common.

Sturbridge laid out its town green right at the time of its establishment in 1738. As part of the expansive yet intimately cozy Sturbridge Common Historic District, the town common area, in addition to the Publick House, features the 1922 Federated Church, 1838 Greek Revival Town Hall, and the 1896 Joshua Hyde Public Library. All this and more led to the district being listed on the National Register of Historic Places in 1977. Many Federal- and Greek

**Sturbridge's town green is mostly unobstructed, making for a scenic place to unwind.**

Revival-style homes are exceptionally well-maintained and date back to the early- to mid-eighteenth century.

Interestingly enough, the town green is nothing spectacular. It has a gazebo and nice expanse of green grass, but that's about it. What elevates the Sturbridge town common into Massachusetts town green greatness, however, is its location surrounded by all those magnificent old New England buildings and homes—with many of the approximately twenty dwellings showcasing a well-maintained Colonial style. The Sturbridge Common Historic District and its town green are every much a requisite stop as Old Sturbridge Village—or any other New England travel attraction, as the overwhelmingly charming authenticity will connect you instantly with small-town New England. Additionally, the town common and historic district, located in a valley between two hills, add a sense of scenic quaintness belying the fact that Worcester—the second-most populated city in New England—is only eighteen miles away.

The Sturbridge Common Historic District and its town green get great use out of its area, perhaps better than most small towns in Massachusetts. Notable events in and around the Sturbridge Town Common include the Thursday night summer Concerts of the Common, the St. Anne–St. Patrick Parishes Apple Bazaar & Carnival in September, the annual Rise & Run Road Race in October, Sturbridge Federated Church Annual Auction in August, Roots N' Bluegrass Festival in September, and the annual Harvest Festival in October.

Also featured in the town green area: the holiday tree-lighting ceremony the last Friday in November and the Sturbridge Winter Family Festival the second Saturday of December.

# SUDBURY

The Sudbury town common doesn't have the historical notoriety of nearby Lexington and Concord, but then again, what towns do? This absolutely charming traditional New England neighborhood is part of a town incorporated that also shares a vital role as a significantly historic town green.

Sudbury contributed a significant number of militia during King Philip's War and was the site of a native raid, according to the "King Philip's War" and "Sudbury Fight" pages of the Town of Sudbury website (www.sudbury.ma.us/services/seniorcenter/custom/hal/kpwar .htm#P1).

Sudbury militia participated in the Battle of Lexington and Concord, in 1775, when Sudbury members attacked British Redcoats returning to Boston. On April 19, 1775, Sudbury's Minutemen gathered at First Parish, known then as the West Side meetinghouse, on the town green. Captain John Nixon led the company, and they fought at the Battles of Lexington and Concord.

Sudbury, incorporated in 1639, saw its first permanent Colonial settlements take place in 1638, with the number of Colonial men, women, and children who were permanent residents of Sudbury in early 1639 about 130, according to the Town of Sudbury website's "A Brief History of the Town of Sudbury, MA, U. S. A" page (www .sudbury.ma.us/services/seniorcenter/custom/hal/sudbury.htm#Hist1). Additionally, Sudbury became the nineteenth Colonial, permanent "Town" within the 1639 boundaries of the Massachusetts Bay Colony. Interestingly enough, this original version of Sudbury was much larger

**The holiday season at the Sudbury town green draws one right into the traditional New England spirit.** SALLY PURRINGTON HILD, EXECUTIVE DIRECTOR, SUDBURY HISTORICAL SOCIETY

geographically than the square mileage seen today, with most of Wayland and Maynard in the mix.

Additional but earlier proof of the Sudbury Center Historic District's deep-rooted history: the Haynes Garrison site, just east of the town center, honors the people of Sudbury who defended their lives and frontier settlements against the allied Indian forces of Philip of Pokanoket.

Taking in the town green area serves as a true local history lesson that might be well-known to locals but deserves to be seen by outsiders. It's about as "New England" as New England gets, with a look that embodies enough history to fill a book (and often has). The National Register of Historic Places listed in 1976 eighty historic buildings over the district's 193 acres, including the Loring Parsonage (c. 1700), the First Parish Meetinghouse (1797), several nineteenth-century buildings, and the Revolutionary Cemetery. The Hosmer House (1793) features splendid mid-nineteenth-century Revival, late-nineteenth- and twentieth-century Revivals, and Federal architecture styles, according to the "*Sudbury's Historic Districts*" section on the Town of Sudbury's website (www.sudbury.ma.us/committees/ historicdistricts/custom/historicdistricts.asp).

Revolutionary War remembrances saturate the Sudbury Historic District and the town, in general, with a dedicated Sudbury Ancient Fyfe and Drum Companie, as well as the Sudbury Companies of Militia & Minute, who use weapons and wear 1775-style clothing to reenact the Battles of Lexington and Concord each year on April 19, according to a Town of Sudbury website page at www.sudbury.ma.us/ services/seniorcenter/custom/hal/sudbury.htm.

"I always enjoyed going up to the center in the early morning of April 19 to watch the militia step off for Concord and Lexington," says Sudbury resident Perry Lowell.

Sally Purrington Hild, executive director of the Sudbury Historical Society, says "Historically, town commons were defined by the fact that they were tracts of land owned by a collective group of townspeople. Shared activities occurred there. What I love about Sudbury's town common is that it still serves as a representative place for all 'Sudburyites,' right in the heart of town. History happens here at our historic town center campus."

Sudbury tries to keep that historical element intact whenever possible.

"I seem to recall that Sudbury was one of the first towns in the area to bury the power lines to make the old town center appear as it did in Colonial times," says Sudbury native Thomas Colantuono.

Current history remains true traditionally to form, too, with such special seasonal events like the Christmas Eve bell ringers playing carols on the steps of the Unitarian church. Also, at Christmas the garden club decorates rooms in the Hosmer House based on a different theme each year. The house is then open to the public for viewing, according to resident Colette Styffe Lankau.

Locals love the town, but often keep coming back to the town green as the center of their close-knit community blessings. Susan Murphy proudly shares some of those elements, reminiscing, "Camp Fire Girls, Girl Scouts, Boy Scouts, Cub Scouts, 4H, Brownies, Blue Birds . . . gathering there together on holidays such as Memorial Day to plant flowers on the graves of veterans, and parades starting or ending there again with floats from most town groups, events like square dancing for all ages held there."

Thomas Colantuono adds this humorous Sudbury town green anecdote: "On April 19, 1975, to celebrate the two hundredth anniversary of the Battles of Lexington and Concord, our family woke up well before dawn and walked the approximate one-half mile to the town center to see the Sudbury Militia march off to Concord. After it was over and we were headed home, my mother asked us what we wanted for breakfast. My brother, who was only six at the time, piped up and said, 'Let's not have English muffins today, how about French toast?'"

For those looking to move to a classic New England town setting, you get more than a town common and some beautiful old homes in the Sudbury Center Historic District. Neighborhood Scout, a research business that analyzes every city and neighborhood in the United States, states of Sudbury's town center district (www.neighborhood scout.com/ma/sudbury/town-center/):

Sudbury Town Center is among the best neighborhoods for families in Massachusetts. In fact, this neighborhood is more family-friendly than 99.5% of neighborhoods in the entire state of Massachusetts. Its combination of top public schools, low crime rates, and owner-occupied single family homes gives this area the look and feel of a "Leave It to Beaver" episode. Many other families also live here, making it easy to socialize and develop a strong sense of community. In addition, the high number of college-educated parents influences the academic success of the local schools.

Although this book focuses on Massachusetts town greens and, often, the historic districts in which they reside, this section on Sudbury would not be complete without two fascinating anecdotes that center around history outside the historic district.

The Wayside Inn, originally known as Howe's Tavern from 1716 to 1861, stands as a beloved landmark attraction as the setting for a group of fictitious characters gathering at the tavern in Henry Wadsworth Longfellow's renowned 1862 book of poems, *Tales of a Wayside Inn*. Howe's Tavern soon changed its name to Longfellow's Wayside Inn, and the rest is history—legendary dining and lodging, a place on the National Register of Historic Places, and tours of the inn as well as the on-site Wayside Gristmill and Redstone School, built by automobile icon Henry Ford (who bought the inn in 1923). Today the Wayside Inn is old, charming, architecturally imperfect, and historic and is filled with rustic rooms, cozy firelight, and New England personalities in period-clothing, circa 1716, intent on serving the best Yankee pot roast and other New England fare known to humankind. The inn and restaurant are located just four miles from the Sudbury town green at 72 Wayside Inn Road.

Major League Baseball legend Babe Ruth also has ties to Sudbury, regarding the town as a "hall of fame" caliber getaway. *Sudbury, 1890–1989, 100 years in the Life of a Town* (Chapter 6) states:

> Ruth discovered Sudbury not long after he joined the Red Sox as a hitting pitcher in the spring of 1914. Several veteran Red Sox players, including his catcher, Chet Thomas, rented or

owned camps in the Pine Lakes area where they could fish, hunt and party without being disturbed. By 1919, Ruth was using a camp on Willis Lake owned by sports enthusiast Larry Joyce. He continued to come to Sudbury even after he was traded to Jacob Ruppert's New York Yankees that winter.

Sudbury, just twenty-five miles from Boston and about a fifteen- to twenty-minute drive to Lexington and Concord, is surely a must-see historical town. Start at the town common and visit the Sudbury Historical Society (call for hours at 978-443-3747) on the second floor of Town Hall in Sudbury Center at the intersection of Old Sudbury Road (MA 27) and Concord Road.

# SUTTON

Very few suburban Massachusetts communities remain true to form due to urban sprawl affecting outlying communities to varying degrees. One look at Sutton, however, and this Worcester suburb resoundingly refutes any notion that oversaturation of commercial and industrial elements permeates all suburbs.

While residential development has increased over the years, the rural template of farms, open land, and a slower pace of life has enjoyed a grand union with Sutton for a long time and most likely for the long-term due to strict zoning laws and dedication to conservation.

A good way to capture Sutton's flavor starts with the Sutton Center Historic District, which includes 435 acres and a great little town common. That town common, along with a burial ground, began in 1719 after the township's settlement in 1716. Typical of an early New England settlement, virtually all the town's civic and institutional buildings are situated around the town common. They include the 1829 Congregational Church and Rufus Putnam Hall, an 1824 school building and Masonic lodge that is now the local history museum. Although built in 1983, Sutton Town Hall resides on the site where the first town hall was built in 1885. The Sutton Center Historic District's only major commercial building is the 1839 Federal-style Brick Block. The building is distinctive as it is the only brick structure in the district. Although not definitely known, some homes near the common go back to the middle of the eighteenth century or earlier. In the historic district many of the

**The Sutton bandstand is surrounded by old homes and some remaining farmland.**

residential and rural properties exhibit diverse architectural styles from the eighteenth to twentieth centuries, including many nine-teenth-century farm outbuildings.

# TAUNTON

Taunton, one of the oldest communities in the United States—founded in 1637 by members of the Plymouth Colony—is a bustling southeastern Massachusetts city that has its social challenges but also myriad reminders of the community's innate grandeur as a community once known as a significant silver-manufacturing center. The silver-manufacturing industry might be the one industry associated with Taunton's earlier day prosperity, but the community also possessed two other industries going all the way back to the 1600s: first, as one of the most successful ironworks towns in the 1600s and then as a ship-building center in the late 1600s. Taunton—with its location on the Taunton River leading out to Mount Hope Bay—actually became one of the most successful, busiest inland seaports on the Atlantic Coast, according to the Old Colony Historical Society Museum website (www.oldcolonyhistoricalsociety.org/society/history).

The Old Colony Museum also states that "the Taunton River also supplied hydraulic power for the many factories and textile mills that operated during the 18th and 19th centuries."

Perhaps the most prominent example of the city's best preservation is the Taunton Green Historic District. It's town common, dating back to 1830, and approximately twenty buildings on fifty acres were all added to the National Register of Historic Places in 1985. Sadly, though, arsonists destroyed historic Templar's Hall (c. 1850) and Cohannet Block (1870) (also known as the Seeley Building) located at the Taunton Green and Weir Street, according to a December 30, 2004 article in the *Taunton Daily Gazette*.

**The Taunton Green Historic District is, not surprisingly, listed on the National Register of Historic Places.**

The Taunton Historic Green has traditionally been the gathering place for troops headed to war. Taunton served as a prominent location in King Philip's War, as well as later leading the colonies in Revolutionary activities, when citizens gathered on the green on October 21, 1774, according to the Old Colony Historical Society. Those citizens raised the Liberty and Union Flag upon a 112-foot Liberty Pole, in defiance of the king. Some call it "the first American flag," as it "still flies from Taunton flagpoles today and celebrates its own annual holiday," according to the Old Colony Historical Society.

Old Colony adds that Taunton has "distinguished itself" in all of our nation's armed conflicts. At or near the Taunton Green stand monuments to the soldiers of all the wars in which "Tauntonians" have participated. This is fitting, as beautiful Taunton Green, now a park, was originally laid out as a training field for the militia in 1639.

The city common is the location for Taunton's annual holiday light display, which is regarded as one of the best of its kind in New England. Since its inception in the early twentieth century, the Taunton Green Christmas display has brought in more than two million people to take in the incredible light displays and other holiday decorations. While Taunton's most prominent nickname is "The Silver City" because of its jewelry-manufacturing roots, its famous Christmas display has resulted in the community also being known as "The Christmas City."

After years of decline, Taunton has rebounded well, with many locally owned downtown stores and a growing restaurant scene leading the way. That, coupled with some of the nicest Colonial and Victorian homes in southeastern Massachusetts along the downtown's east side of Route 44, make for a city once again full of promise and a town common that has remained beautiful throughout the ups and downs of this close-knit small city. 🪶

# TEMPLETON

Don't go looking for anything extra in Templeton, other than a beautiful town common, nice old homes, and really down-to-earth people. Come to think of it, isn't that all we need in life? The rest is just gravy!

A small north-central Massachusetts town with little industry and minimal commercial endeavors, the Templeton Common Historic District encompasses Athol, Gardner, Hubbardston, Dudley, Wellington, and South Roads and a truly nice town green. What stands out is the gazebo juxtaposed with the historic First Church of Templeton. With a 1983 designation on the National Register of Historic Places, the Templeton Common Historic District is not just about the town green but also pleasing homes of varying architectural styles reportedly dating back as far as 1760 (on Dolbear Hill by Zacchius Barrett; the second home, the Joshua Wright Tavern, in 1763), according to the "Templeton Center" page on the Town of Templeton's website (www.templeton1.org/home/slideshows/templeton-center). Historical homes and buildings include the aforementioned First Church of Templeton, originally erected as the town's meetinghouse in 1811; the Silas Stone house (1770); the Boynton Public Library (1885); Blodgett Building, originally built by Artemas Lee in 1829 (now Templeton's Ice Cream Barn and the Country Store, as well as apartments); the Landlord's Inn, built on the site of the Templeton Inn in 1900, now the site of the Templeton Center Fire Station; and Grange Hall (1897).

The Narragansett Historical Society—also known as the Templeton Historical Society—has served as a wonderful resource for town history since 1924, as well as a town green–area gathering place for

This scene of the First Church of Templeton and bandstand highlights a simply beautiful Templeton town common.

various seasonal events. Some of those events include teas, craft shows, kite days, and engine displays.

Templeton is one of the few towns where you won't find much information online—either an inconvenience, or a revelation in a world that has become part of the Internet revolution. Townsfolk feel no need to tell the world about their beautiful little town, and it is this modesty that creates the magic behind a small New England town. Gathering around the town green for events and living in historic homes create a wonderful quality of life, indeed, for Templeton residents, who clearly thrive on the simple things in life.

# WAKEFIELD

This suburb north of Boston stands as the only "lake town" in eastern Massachusetts—that is, having a downtown situated on a large lake. This waterfront presence allows for an absolutely beautiful town common setting. While the attractive Upper Common hugs the splendid "Main Street USA" look of the downtown, the adjacent Lower Common is located on the hard-to-pronounce-but-easy-to-enjoy Lake Quannapowitt—initially formed when a glacial ice block broke away from a main glacier. With a historic bandstand and large expanse of green space, the laid-back Lower Common lake scene looks more like a scenic Upstate New York town than the Boston suburbs. The Lower Common also hooks up with a paved sidewalk that spans the four-mile lake, thus making it a perfect place to walk. Additionally, thousands turn out for summer concerts on the common and the largest Fourth of July parade in Massachusetts. The Festival by the Lake—held by the Wakefield Center Neighborhood Association—is another major Lower Common event held the second Saturday in June, featuring crafters, artists, musical entertainment, local organizations, and food.

Nancy Bertrand, of the Wakefield Historical Society, says, "The story of Wakefield Common is a bit complicated. First of all, Wakefield is actually the earliest part of the town now known as Reading."

She explains that when Reading was first incorporated in 1644, it actually included all of Wakefield and all of North Reading, as well as what is now Reading. The town of Wakefield broke off from the town of Reading in 1812 and incorporated as the Town of South Reading.

**Lake Quannapowitt provides the perfect setting for a town common.**

Finally, Wakefield became officially incorporated in 1868. So, the town common came before the incorporation of Wakefield.

Bertrand says that the remains of the original town green, established in the 1640s, are present in what is now the Upper Common. The common was originally a wide expanse that stretched down to the present Water Street—thus explaining why Main Street is so wide. What is now called the Lower Common was not part of the original common—it was added as a public park much later, according to Bertrand.

The original town common held a schoolhouse on it, along with hayscales and a blacksmith shop through much of the eighteenth and nineteenth centuries. Cattle grazed upon the common, says Bertrand, but cattle grazing was regulated in 1656. In 1665 a herdsman was appointed to care for cattle grazing upon the common land. (In 1725, an ordinance was enacted forbidding geese on the common, but allowing swine.)

Bertrand says that the town green was not the primary military training ground in the seventeenth century, but used for some military training and rallies in the nineteenth century. Conveniently, Hale's Tavern was located adjacent to the common during the War of 1812, allowing for refreshments after the rallies.

The common also has included, at various times in its history, a Liberty Tree, a portable bandstand, and a skating pond. Bertrand adds that "our history also notes that an unpopular employer was at one time hanged—in effigy—upon the Common."

In 1885, after receiving a bequest from a Wakefield native, the town acted to purchase the land that is now called the Lower Common. (At the time of its establishment, however, it was called Wakefield Park; the "Common" designation came later.) Soon afterward, the bandstand was built. Its presence looks simply lovely by the lake.

The Upper Common (the remains of the original Common) is the site of the Soldiers & Sailors Monument, dedicated in 1902 to Civil War servicemen. Over the years, monuments to servicemen and -women in other wars and conflicts were added to the common, making it the "Veterans' Memorial Common," according to Bertrand.

The common has been the site of rallies and community meetings for many important town and national events, from the celebration of the change of the town's name to Wakefield in 1868 to the many large-scale concerts and festivals commemorating the town's 350th anniversary in 1994, according to Bertrand.

She adds that since the establishment of the Lower Common, most of these gatherings take place there. "The Lower Common is a busy place—it is the location of many fundraising events, most notably our annual Festival by the Lake, which takes place annually in June," says Bertrand. "In addition, Wakefield allows many nonprofit and charity groups and organizations conducting fundraising walks and runs around Lake Quannapowitt (a perfect 5K fitness walk/run) to use the Lower Common. And of course, we have our annual July fourth celebrations."

While the Lower Common possesses the best scenery given its blessed location, the Upper Common is no slouch, either, with its attractive spring flower beds, period lighting, benches, and very well-maintained paved walkways and several dedication monuments. Together they create a town-green combination that is a joy to visit, with its lake location, a thriving downtown, and myriad events.

# WALPOLE

Walpole, a likable mid-size town eighteen miles southwest of Boston, is a classic New England mill town (established in 1724), with its industrial roots planted firmly in the former grist mills, clothing mills, farming-tool manufacturing plants, and cotton factories. Today Walpole looks quaint and historic, with most of the mills and factories either gone or nicely used for, largely, modern-day commercial use. The town also happens to possess one of the most unusual town common presences in Massachusetts. Not one, but three town commons comprise a good portion of the downtown and get put to good use through myriad dedication sites, as well as seasonal events including Memorial and Veterans Day observances, parts of Walpole Town Day in May, the Epiphany Parish of Walpole Annual Village Fair (across the street from the common) in June, a summer farmers' market, and a tree-lighting ceremony and Santa's visit on the Saturday after Thanksgiving.

The three town commons have resulted from, no doubt, parcels of land being broken up for development purposes. Clearly straying from its original 1739 presence, the town commons, nevertheless, stand today as three distinct properties that still lend a spaciousness to the downtown area—a rarity in suburban Boston towns. The common area reportedly served as a gathering place for American soldiers, as in 1775 Walpole sent 157 men to the Battle of Lexington and Concord. A longtime Walpole resident also told me that he believes two National Guard units gathered at the town green in preparation for World War II. The town common once also was used as a place for animals to graze and horses to drink from the fountain on Common

**A stone gazebo, with the United Church of Walpole in the background, offers a welcoming scene at the town green.**

Street. Most of the town common's history, however, has seen its land used as a community gathering place for social purposes.

Walpole's first meetinghouse was established in 1739 and located on what is now the town common. That meetinghouse was torn down in 1783 for a new one, but eventually separation of church and state led to the house being taken off the property.

Dedication sites include a memorial to Walpole soldiers of the French and Indian War of 1754; a 1936 cross commemorating where Walpole's first "houses of God" stood at the "Old Meetinghouse Common"; a soldiers memorial to THOSE WHO MADE THE SUPREME SACRIFICE IN ALL WARS DURING THE 20TH CENTURY; a flagpole and plaque dedicated to World War II veteran Everett A. "Rocky" Rockwood (Nov. 21, 1924–Jan. 5, 2013); a firefighters' memorial; and benches memorializing World War II veterans.

As a true testimony to the town's respect for those who have served, the Common Street town common features the 1903 C. S. Bird Fountain, which was restored and then dedicated in 2008 to

Army First Lieutenant Andrew Bacevich, who was killed on May 13, 2007, by an improvised explosive device while deployed in Iraq. As a truly generous incentive, the Veterans Development Corporation, of Norwell, Massachusetts, volunteered all the necessary materials and labor to restore the former historic C. S. Bird Fountain in Bacevich's name.

A charming stone gazebo dating back to 1901 stands out as a one-of-a-kind structure on the town green. The gazebo looks virtually unchanged since its inception, with the exception of wrought-iron railings added in the 1970s for safety purposes. The gazebo has a rather fascinating history, as so well stated in David Levine's "A Secret Jewel, History Stands Still" blog (with information gathered by the late Elizabeth Cottrell of Walpole). Joseph Feely, a representative of Walpole's Improvement Association, had the gazebo constructed—with town approval, of course—and gave it as a gift to the town (his name is affixed to the structure). President John F. Kennedy and his wife Jacqueline came to Walpole during his campaign for president and spoke to locals from the gazebo. As a token of appreciation from his legion of Walpole supporters, Kennedy reportedly received flowers from Gallo Florists and candy from Watson's Candy (still in business!). As an interesting side note and ode to "ye olde" celebrity sightings, many famous historical figures most likely discovered the town common as stagecoaches passed through the town—perhaps between thirty and forty daily—including that transporting French General Lafayette and General George Washington. Also, a member of the Bonaparte family, a brother of the first Napoleon, is said to have ridden through. Why that occurred we'll never know! Alexander Hamilton, John Quincy Adams, General Andrew Jackson, Martin Van Buren, and many other dignitaries also traveled through Walpole.

Today the bandstand serves as a location for musicians to perform during the Tuesday summer concert on the common series, and as a location for dignitaries to speak at events—most notably on Memorial and Veterans Day. Former US Senator Scott Brown, who once resided a few towns over in Wrentham, spoke from the bandstand to Walpole residents during the 2010 Veterans Day Ceremony.

From Front Street, the town commons all seem to blend together, almost creating a parklike appearance. With beautiful landscaping, well-maintained open green spaces, paved walkways, period lighting, and the gazebo, the chance to walk all three town commons evokes a true feeling of quintessential New England. Churches, shops and restaurants, and historic municipal and privately owned buildings surround the town commons and add a wonderful almost modern-day Mayberry RFD vibe to the town. In addition, the chance to shop and eat right across the street from the town green is a huge plus, as many small Massachusetts communities with town greens have very little to do other than walk the common. Additionally, Walpole has the highest concentration of residents of Irish descent, at nearly 40 percent of the town's entire population, so to no surprise, there's an added "green" element to the Walpole town green: three authentic Irish pubs—Finnegan's Wake, The Raven's Nest, and Napper Tandy's—within two hundred yards of the town commons!

Pam Driscoll, a lifelong Walpole resident, knows the common well and has some wonderful, often emotional, memories of good and bad times around the Walpole town green:

> Most of my memories of the common are connected with the Epiphany Church of Walpole, as I've been going there since 1978. The common was always an extension of our church. I remember my parents taking us over to Mimi's Variety Store and we got to pick out one donut each and then we would all go as a family after church and sit on the common and eat our donuts—that was our one treat of the week.
>
> We also gathered at the common after both my sister and brother's weddings, the baptisms of my children, and the funerals of my father and grandfather. It's such a peaceful place—not very large—but, nonetheless, just the right size to be together with family. Most recently I took our puppy around the common and church grounds for his first walk in Massachusetts. He's a rescue from Tennessee. CJ, our puppy, and I also sit at the common every week while my daughter Jackie is at piano lessons.

Dan Ryan, also a lifelong resident, remembers as a kid eating homemade chocolates by the bandstand on the town common.

"My fondest memory of the center of town as a kid was going to Watson's candy store and watching my grandmother, Isabella Boivin, hand dip candy in chocolate," says Ryan. "[I] used to go to the bandstand and eat over there."

Sam Obar, one of the youngest and more active Walpole Town Meeting members, says, "Our town common is a wonderful focal point of our downtown, and we are extraordinarily fortunate to have a town green."

No matter what time of day, there always seems to be someone at the town common, as families, town employees on work break, business travelers, and all walks of life take full advantage of the great walking opportunities through the common and Common Street as a popular addition to the walk. This classic American street is right up there with famous New England streets in towns like Lexington and Concord, with its amazing concentration of large Colonials, Victorians, Federal Greek Revivals, and farmhouses—many with large front lawns. They include the following:

- 1875 Colonel William Moore House at 45 Common Street
- 1830 Washington Glover House at 64 Common Street
- 1825 Clapp-Cobb House at 103 Common Street
- 1827 Calvin G. Hartshorn House at 118 Common Street

Also, the Walpole Historical Society is located right off the common, at the 1826 Deacon Willard Lewis House on 33 West Street. As of this writing, the society is open most Saturdays from 2 to 4 p.m.

Walpole is known as the "Friendly Town," and the best place to feel that welcoming nature is by starting at the town green and working your way from there. The Boston area perhaps undeservedly gets a bad rap for being cold and impersonal, but you'd never know it in Walpole. It almost has a welcoming Midwest "salt-of-the-earth" heartland personality with an added traditional New England look!

# WALTHAM

Driving down Main Street in Waltham reveals a wall of commercial and industrial buildings with no end in sight. All of a sudden, however, this wall-to-wall urban scene gives way virtually out-of-the-blue to an oasis of much-needed open space at the classic Waltham Common. Once walking into the Waltham town green, there's almost an instant feeling of being far away from the hustle and bustle of the city. The dense urban landscapes give way to a 6.34-acre city green with densely populated trees, multiple paved pathways, and a Colonial Revival–style city hall with a limestone facade, built in 1926, dedicated in 1927, and located on its own rectangular piece of land next to the town common. At the outside of the town common on Main Street stands a huge clock.

The Waltham Town Common, bounded by Carter, Moody, Main, and Elm Streets, is a significant part of the Waltham Central Square Historic District that includes the 1887 fire station that features a Queen Anne–style architecture and a police station built in 1890 designed by Hartwell & Richardson, according to the Massachusetts Cultural Resource Information System Central Square Historic District nomination form for the National Register of Historic Places. That architectural firm contributed significantly to the current architecture of the greater Boston area.

The Waltham town green also features four monuments: a granite obelisk from 1867 with urn designed by Boston architect George Meacham; a statue dedicated in 1909 of Nathaniel Prentice Banks, a former Massachusetts governor and American Civil War general designed by Henry Hudson Kitson; and "The Hiker," a memorial to

The Waltham city common bandstand sits at the forefront here, close to Waltham City Hall.

veterans of the Spanish–American War created by Kitson's wife Theodora, dedicated sometime in the early twentieth century.

The Waltham Central Square Historic District was placed on the National Register of Historic Places in 1989. This is a rather interesting designation, as although Waltham was settled in 1634 and incorporated as a town in 1738, there was really no downtown district until the mid-1800s. Just a few towns over from Boston, Waltham has grown tremendously in a short of amount of time—including the downtown district, the famous and relevant technology beltway right off I-95, a dedication to higher education as home to Bentley

College and Brandeis University, and lots of post–World War II home development. But Waltham still has a significant amount of open space, including the four hundred–acre Lyman Estate and Prospect Hill—the second-highest elevation in the Boston area next to the Blue Hills in the Canton/Milton area.

Waltham Day on the Common is one of the most popular events at the town green, usually held the third Saturday in September. The community event features "food, fun, music, and tables" and "quizzes for kids about nature in Waltham and pulled bittersweet vines to twist into wreaths," according to the event's creator, the Waltham Land Trust. From July to August, the Waltham Arts Council offers free concerts on the Waltham Common. Music includes contemporary, jazz, '50s and '60s, country, pop, and big band. The annual tree-lighting ceremony takes place, usually the third Friday of November, with holiday singing and a mailbox set up where Santa can receive his mail (Santa's office is at Waltham City Hall during the holiday season).

One final thought: The Waltham Town Common has a location convenient to a revitalized downtown district with a vibrant restaurant scene (known as "Restaurant Row" on Moody Street) with just about every type of food available, as well as book stores, a movie theater, an ice-cream shop, and a diversity of other locally owned mom-and-pop stores. It's still a work in progress, but nevertheless, one of the more impressive downtown districts in the Greater Boston area.

# WENDELL

Wendell, first settled in 1754 and officially incorporated in 1781, is one of New England's great hidden towns—so pretty and welcoming and without an air of pretentiousness. Located in north-central Massachusetts, the town's center features marvelous historical preservation—at the Wendell Town Common Historic District, listed on the Massachusetts Register of Historic Places—including a one-acre rectangular town common that dates back to 1774.

The Wendell Common was officially deeded to the town in 1789 by early settler and deacon of the Congregational church Jonathan Osgood. It was intended to be used as a place for cattle to graze and for a military training field, according to local historian Pam Richardson.

While the town common doesn't get as much daily usage as it did a generation ago when "dads and their sons were out on the town common playing baseball," according to Richardson, the open space does have some special seasonal events. Old Home Day—possibly dating back to the late 1800s—takes place the third Saturday in August and features music, food, arts and crafts, local business vendors, and plenty of kids' activities. Originally created as an event to welcome back those who left Wendell, Old Home Day in its current format is essentially a town day event that draws in mostly current residents.

"It's our big event," says Richardson with lots of pride.

Then there's the fall harvest dinner that, one year, took place on the town common, but was moved to the Town Hall (formerly the old Baptist church), across from the town green, because of the "chill in the air," according to Richardson.

**Fall foliage meets the Wendell town green.**

The farmers' market has been a recent success, says Richardson, taking place on Saturday during the summer. Occasionally other events will occur on the town common, like a local "Tai Chi teacher bringing her lessons outside," says Richardson.

The town common—split into two sections by Morse Village Road—also features memorials to local soldiers who served in World War I, World War II, and Vietnam. Many years ago locals planted a maple tree on the town green in honor of the tragedy that occurred with the Fukushima Daiichi nuclear disaster, initiated primarily by the tsunami in 2011. Also on the town green: a "free box" next to the meetinghouse where people can drop off clothes for those in need.

"I think most people in Wendell have at least one piece of clothing from that box!" says Richardson.

Opposite the town common are predominantly early nineteenth-century buildings with Greek Revival–style architecture, according to the Commonwealth of Massachusetts Inventory Record for the Wendell Town Common. Richardson believes that a local lumberman, Luke Leach, was responsible for building many of the Greek Revival homes—and possibly the 1846 Congregational Church (no longer in use but with a recent town-wide move to have it restored for other uses). The Wendell Baptist Church was built in 1819, then dismantled, moved to its current location on the common, and rebuilt in 1846. According to Richardson's research, George B. Richardson (chair maker, carpenter, and, at various times, selectman, town clerk, and deacon of the Baptist church) is the man who both donated the site on the common and rebuilt the church.

"I cannot find any description of the building in the papers that were submitted to the Massachusetts Historical Commission, so I cannot definitively give you its architectural style," says Richardson. "However, it has standard Greek Revival features which, I assume, were part of the design changes made in its reconstruction."

There's only one twentieth-century building of historical significance—the Wendell Free Library built in 1921 with a Colonial Revival style.

The district was listed on the National Register of Historic Places in 1992. No stores or other commercial businesses exist in the central district. A quarter mile "down the road," according to Richardson, is a pub, country store, and post office.

Richardson says that because Wendell was a "poor town" in its developmental stages, many homes succumbed to fires—thus reducing the number of historic homes near the town common. Today Wendell is a modest but more robust community with many younger people moving into town in search of small-town life, greater affordability, and the chance to connect to the land with farming. Richardson says there is a bit of a "hippie" vibe to the town and that "no other town in the area has this type of feel."

Wendell's population peaked in the 1850s at one thousand, and only until recently has the number of residents returned to that level. Clearly many have rediscovered this pure and welcoming hidden town with the beautiful town common!

# WEST BOYLSTON

First settled in 1642 and incorporated in 1808, West Boylston stands as one of the older communities in Massachusetts. The town common still represents a dedicated, traditional community gathering place, as it is located in the center of a close-knit small town. Walking around the central district and the town green, in particular, you'd never know that Worcester—the second-most populated city in New England—is located just fifteen minutes away.

Interestingly enough, the town green you see today isn't the original West Boylston center, as a few miles away is the town's reservoir, which now covers the town's original center as well as Main Street, according to the West Boylston High School website (http://viscomm.wbschools.com/community2012kunz.htm). The site also states that "when the area was originally flooded, this town common was unofficially substituted."

Incorporated in 1808, West Boylston evolved into a town that thrived on textile and other industries and was greatly affected by the making of the Wachusett Reservoir upon its completion in 1905. The West Boylston Historical Society website's history page at www.wbhistory.org/history.htm states, "Because of the water power available from three rivers at the south branch of the Nashua, the Stillwater and the Quinapoxet, many more mills would follow and the center of town would move north to the area now across the causeway."

**The Town of West Boylston's bell rings a nice tone at the town green.**

Local landowner Squire Ezra Beaman—also a major in the Revolutionary War—helped break off Boylston from Shrewsbury in 1786. But locals grew tired of living in Boylston, as taking a horse and buggy seven miles to church probably was the Colonial version of trying to tolerate modern traffic gridlocks in Boston—that is, too inconvenient and frustrating.

After failed attempts to separate the town, Ezra had a "revolutionary" idea: call a meeting of the people of the western part of town and volunteer to pay for building a new meetinghouse, according to the West Boylston Historical Society website (www.wbhistory.org). The Historical Society states, "Construction began in 1793, and the new church was dedicated on the site of the present Congregational Church on New Year's Day, 1795. In 1796, this area, after considerable objection from Boylston, was chartered as the Second Parish and Second Precinct of Boylston, Sterling and Holden."

With precinct status granted in 1796, West Boylston eventually became officially incorporated in 1796.

That move paved the way for a truly attractive small town to develop, including the town common. Because of its classic New England town common look, the West Boylston town green remains one of the most photographed of its kind in central Massachusetts. The town green also features many events, including the West Boylston Fall Fest held typically in early October; the tree-lighting ceremony in early December; and the Summer Bandstand Concert Program at the gazebo on Sunday evening.

Seasonal events do not tell the whole modern-day town green story, however. West Boylston Historical Society volunteer Don De-Marsh says that locals, in the finest New England tradition, use the town green on a daily basis.

"It's a very traditional place," says DeMarsh. "People frequently stroll here, walk their dogs and kids play all the time."

West Boylston's close-knit neighborhoods play a major role in the town green still being used as a gathering place, but DeMarsh adds, "the location helps, too. There's lots of traffic around the area at the intersection of Routes 140 and 12. It's hard to miss the town common."

The Congregational Church and many other historic homes give the West Boylston town green added authenticity to the town common area, including a "white house that was once a distillery and a building formerly serving as a meetinghouse and general store," according to DeMarsh. Dedication sites include a ground-level bell in honor of Julius F. Lovell, who was West Bolylston's auditor from 1934 to 1935, a selectman from 1935 to 1941, and town moderator from 1942 to 1959; and memorial sites dedicated to soldiers from West Boylston.

The West Boylston Historical Society, at 65 Worcester Road (508-835-6971), is located right off the town green and serves as an active resource for townsfolk and visitors. Staying true to form, the West Boylston Historical Society is housed in what was originally the Bigelow Tavern—built in the 1770s by Deacon Amariah Bigelow for his son Abel, who was the first innkeeper, according to the Historical Society website. In addition to providing historical information, the Historical Society also has created a museum on the premises with a library, a reading room, work rooms, and display space. Call for hours and definitely make the West Boylston Historical Society part of your visit to the town green!

# WEST BROOKFIELD

Although West Brookfield possesses a beautiful town common, it would do injustice to the town just to focus solely on that much-revered open space. Located on a quiet stretch of Route 9 in central Massachusetts's unspoiled Quaboag Valley just twenty miles west of Worcester, West Brookfield leaves an immediate serene impression upon a first visit, and repeated visits as well for that matter, with its appealing, historic, off-the-beaten-path, New England small-town presence.

West Brookfield features a stunning, six-acre triangular town green that is generally regarded as one of the prettiest in New England. Three notable attractions grace the common. The most prominent is the Rice Memorial Fountain and the Rice Drinking Fountain, erected in 1886 and given as a gift from former Massachusetts Senator George Rice in memory of his parents, Samuel and Abigail Rice. Set in the center of the town green, the fountain is twenty-three-feet tall and a bright blue-green color. In 1938 the "Lady Atop the Fountain" was destroyed in a hurricane and was restored in 1985 by J. Irving England, according to the West Brookfield Historical Commission. A red brick walkway surrounds the fountain and includes many benches where locals and visitors can relax to the soothing sound of water, breathe in the fresh country air, and be surrounded by the essence of traditional New England with a high concentration of well-kept nineteenth-century homes—most in a Federal- and Greek-style architecture.

The 1886 Rice Memorial Fountain resides in the center of the West Brookfield town green.

The Helen Paige Shackley Bandstand, located on the east side of the common, looks like no other bandstand and proves that town green structures don't have to be old to have charm, as this particular structure was dedicated in 1972. This magnificent bandstand with intricate detail and a freshly painted white look is most prominently used for the Summer Concerts on the Commons event held every Wednesday in July and August.

The War Memorial Plaza—a dedication site to locals who served and paid the ultimate price for protecting our freedoms—sits on the west side entrance of the common and was beautifully built and is now well maintained.

"The West Brookfield common represents town pride and togetherness," says Jasmine Robinson, a West Brookfield native. "Events our little town takes pride in like the Asparagus Festival—the common is abuzz with all ages enjoying visiting neighbors with just as much as shopping and eating. My favorite that has evolved since I was kid in the 1980s is White Christmas, with the spectacular lighting of the giant pine tree! Who needs the Hallmark Channel?! We live that here in West Brookfield! I grew up here. Moved away during college and moved back in my late twenties to settle down and raise a family. The town common and the bond it offers with townsfolk is one of the reasons for moving back!"

One of Timothy Czub's favorite West Brookfield town green memories: "Growing up playing baseball on the common."

Claudia Tytula favors the Concerts on the Common, stating, "The Wednesday night Concerts on the Common have always been a time for the generations to get together and enjoy an evening of music, friendship, and fun."

Barbara Smith, going way back, reflects on her favorite activities: "Playing on the common in the early 1940s, making leave houses, and going to the Fireman's carnival."

Laurel T. Shaw Leslie is a big fan of the West Brookfield town green, especially during autumn and for its timeless qualities: "The common is so beautiful in the fall with all the maple trees ablaze. The common reminds me of all the former settlers who lived here and possibly grazed their livestock on the common. It's a piece of land that connects the past with the present."

But it's not just what's on the West Brookfield town green, but also what surrounds this authentic slice of Americana. Some examples of old, impressive downtown architecture near the town green include the Town Hall built in 1859; the Merriam Gilbert Library dating back to 1880; the Ye Olde Tavern (still operating today for food, drink, and functions) from 1760; and Sacred Heart of Jesus Roman Catholic Church, built in 1889.

The West Brookfield Center Historic District comprises approximately eighty-five acres, according to the West Brookfield Historical Commission, encompassing areas north, south, and west of the common. The Center Historic District features 211 buildings, including a total of "204 houses, barns, outbuildings and stores." This is a remarkable accomplishment, given West Brookfield has a population of under four thousand!

West Brookfield's history is indeed significant. First settled in 1664 and formally incorporated in 1848, West Brookfield was once a halfway stop on the stagecoach route from Worcester to Springfield. West Brookfield also possessed the sites of the "first white settlement, the Indian Villages" as a presence of the "mother town of the Quaboag Plantation, which was deeded in 1660," according to the writings of Amy Dugas—a member of the West Brookfield Historical Commission. Dugas explains that "*Quaboag* is a Nipmuc Indian name meaning 'before the pond' which is Lake Wekabaug in the town."

Additionally, the town has some well-known connections from the past: Lucy Stone, a famous American suffragist, was born in West Brookfield, and Noah Webster published his dictionary here.

About a mile down the road from the town green is the well-known Salem Cross Inn Restaurant. Listed on the National Register of Historic Places, the inn is a remarkable example of Colonial restoration, with its original building constructed in the early 1700s. The handsome hardwood floors, post-and-beam ceilings, roaring fireplaces, antique furnishings, serene candlelight glow, and gracious, old-fashioned "New England" waitresses dressed in Colonial apparel offer a complete feeling of warmth and comfort on three floors of charming old rooms. Some stellar examples of old New England ambiance abound in the Chestnut Room, with its huge fieldstone fireplace and forty-two-feet-long chestnut ceiling beams; the old hay barn, known as the Hexmark Tavern, affording splendid views of the woods and meadows; and, inside, smaller rooms filled with antiquarian books, maps, documents, and other curios. The Salem Cross Inn Restaurant faithfully sticks to traditional New England cooking, with the use of open-hearth fireplaces to slow roast its delicious prime rib and a restored 1699 Bannister Tavern beehive oven to turn out some delicious baked goods and dishes!

Continuing its traditional New England ways, West Brookfield today is big on small-town annual events like the aforementioned Concerts on the Common and many more special community gatherings that bring in visitors from all over New England. The previously mentioned Asparagus and Flower Heritage Festival is usually held the third Saturday in May and fills much of the town green with plants for sale, garden items, pony rides, and raffles, and the Quaboag Historical Society and other local organizations and businesses offer specialty items. Food is a main draw here, with many asparagus-inspired dishes and old standbys like burgers, hot dogs, and baked goods.

An interesting anecdote about West Brookfield is that it is believed to be the birthplace of asparagus, as Diederik Leertouwer lived here with his family between 1704 and 1798 and brought asparagus from his homeland of the Netherlands to cultivate locally!

A Christmas tree-lighting ceremony is held during "White Christmas in West Brookfield," which takes place on the first Saturday of December and features open houses, horse-drawn carriage rides, an elf hunt for the kids, caroling, and more.

West Brookfield is ultimately true New England in its most authentic form. As part of a region called the Brookfields (including West Brookfield, North Brookfield, and East Brookfield), this area perhaps represents the best of traditional small-town Massachusetts with winding country roads, lakes and ponds, apple farms, antiques shops, church fairs, large village greens, and a sense of community spirit and much-welcomed underdevelopment that you thought you'd never see again. West Brookfield resonates as a hidden Massachusetts travel gem, far removed from the twenty-first century in the best sense, with its beautiful tree-lined side streets featuring fine old neighborhoods and scenic, secluded Lake Wickaboag. It is really like going back in time, as further evidenced by families congregating on their front porches, country roads with big farms and open land, and virtually no commercial or industrial development.

"Driving through on a snowy winter evening, the houses with candles in the windows, the tree and bandstand lit, [it's like] something from a Norman Rockwell painting," says Dawn M. Rolla Guzik. "Love this town!"

# WESTFORD

This north-central Massachusetts town has seen tremendous commercial and residential growth in the past twenty-five years, but fortunately the Westford Center Historic District—that includes a pretty town green—has retained a remarkable sense of its 1700s and 1800s heritage. The town green, which was initially used as a military training ground starting in 1748, eventually evolved into a public park to be primarily used for Memorial Day, Veterans Day, and other civic celebrations.

The town green comprises about one acre and has a truly attractive look with grass, trees, and shrubs. History abounds, with markers being placed as early as 1899 (the cannon on the east side of the town common). A 1924 memorial on the town green honors Westford residents serving in the military from the Colonial era through World War I. This eight-sided monument features a bronze eagle and has an entire side dedicated to Westford's Civil War volunteers. There was a bandstand on the common from the 1860s until around 1900 (with locals currently raising funds to build a new one).

Always a town center with minimal commercial activity, it is the historic homes and buildings that wonderfully frame the town common to lend an old-time New England look. Westford Academy (the sole public high school in town) resides most prominently—dating back to 1793.

The Westford Civil War Monument, erected in 1910, stands tall and proud on a piece of land across from the town green and honors more than two hundred men from Westford that served in the Union military during the Civil War.

**New England town greens don't get much nicer than the Westford town common.**

Main town-green events include the First Parish's Annual Pancake Breakfast on Westford Town Common held in mid-May, and the Westford Summer Concerts on the Common typically held on Sunday during July and August.

# WESTON

The price of a home in Weston averages more than a million dollars, so it should come as no surprise that this Metro West Boston suburb's town green looks like a million bucks.

Not your typical New England town common with its deep-rooted history (the town was first settled in 1642 and incorporated in 1713), the Weston town green is a relative newcomer, dating back to 1910 with a goal to create "a village common, or green, always found in the best types of old New England villages," according to the Weston Historical District website (http://westhistcomm.org/districts-and-areas-2/national-register-districts/boston-post-road-historic-district/).

Arthur Shurtleff (later Shurcliff) wrote in the 1912 *Weston Town Report* about the rationale of building the town green: "In my opinion, the execution of this scheme would give Weston a Town Common of remarkable individuality and in many respects the finest open space of its kind in the Commonwealth."

Built around the town common around that period of time were a 1913 fire station and Weston Town Hall (1917)—both in the form of Georgian/Colonial Revival–style architecture—and the Gothic Revival St. Julia Church (1919).

Creating this "new" town center also served as a convenient oasis near the famed Boston Post Road—the route of choice before the Mass Turnpike (Route 90) was ever conceived. It was, in fact, that the Boston Post Road in Weston was one of the first stagecoach stops in the eighteenth century.

Weston's stretch of the Boston Post Road runs three and a half miles east to west from the Waltham line to the Wayland line, as part

**A flag scene lends a spectacular look to the Weston town green.**

of an east–west connector with just a convenient minute's drive to the village green and town center.

Once in the town center, it's easy to get drawn in by the town green. The many families and other local residents—utilizing so well their idyllic-looking open spaces—make the scene look like something out of a Norman Rockwell *Saturday Evening Post* magazine cover.

The Weston Historical Society says it well about their prized possession—the town green—and what surrounds it:

> Since the creation of the Town Green a century ago, Town leaders have carefully protected this centerpiece of the Town.

Lamson Park was taken by eminent domain to protect the visual integrity of the Green and Town Hall. A recent addition to the Town Hall was carefully designed to preserve the character of the building. The exterior of the Josiah Smith Tavern was restored in 2006 with Community Preservation Act funds. First Parish Church has carefully guarded the integrity of its handsome stone building, which has several additions in compatible style. Constraints on the library site meant that the 1899 building was never expanded and it maintains its architectural integrity. As a result, the Town Green area looks much like it did a century ago, when Town leaders completed their visionary Town Improvement Plan. Now, it is up to us to preserve this legacy.

# WHITMAN

Town greens don't always have to be located on Main Street, and Whitman offers a fine example of this. After many years of visiting this midsize southeastern Massachusetts town east of Brockton, it was only recently that I discovered the Whitman town park—or should I say, I found it with a little help from the owner of the old-time Duval's Pharmacy in downtown Whitman. Not being able to find Whitman's town common, I asked Alan Duval about this great piece of open space that several friends had raved about. He took me outside his store and gave verbal directions with some added help from his right hand pointing in various directions. Turns out the town common is located behind Whitman Town Hall and bounded by side streets—Maple Street and Park, Whitman, and Hayden Avenues. It's a fourteen-acre beauty, established in 1880 (when the town was known as Old Abington) as a gift from Augustus Whitman (from the Whitman family that eventually gave the town its name in 1886), with some impressive landscaping and design, courtesy of the famous Olmsted brothers around 1900. The mix of woodlands and open space, a gazebo, a pond with a fountain, benches, multiple paths, a Civil War monument from 1908, a swimming pool, a playground, and a Little League field collectively results in a presence that is unmistakably Americana. To no surprise, the town green is listed on the National Register of Historic Places.

One could argue that the land is a park, but the overall vibe leans toward a classic New England town common with a bandstand, a 1908 Civil War monument, old homes surrounding the land, and a downtown location. The gazebo is of particular historical interest, as

**A view of Whitman town park from the bandstand.**

in 1908 the Department of Public Works of Whitman and the Regal (Shoe) Band, came up with $350 from town funds and another $40 from private donations to construct their "very sturdy bandstand which is gazebo-shaped and is raised on a 6-foot stone and mortar foundation with storage space underneath for removable stairs and equipment," according to information provided by Frank Lyman, of the Whitman Historical Society, that can be found on the History Stands Still website (http://bandstands.blogspot.com/2009/03/whitman-ma .html). The structure was also outfitted with "lighting and provides power receptacles for equipment used during concerts and other events," states Lyman.

Speaking of the downtown, it's worth visiting for its trip-back-in-time look, including head-on parking, Duval's Pharmacy, and the no-frills Venus Cafe at 47 South Street, which has constantly shown up during local "best of" pizza discussions since 1964.

A popular event at Whitman Town Park is the Thursday Night Summer Concert series.

# WILLIAMSTOWN

Generally regarded as one of Massachusetts's most beautiful towns, this community on the New York State border has "quaint, historic, scenic, and academic" written all over it. Ideally situated in the Berkshire Mountains of western Massachusetts, Williamstown is most famous as being home to Williams College (established in 1793)—a highly regarded secondary learning institution that recently earned accolades in the September 9, 2015, *U.S. World and News Report "Best College Rankings"* article as the number-one National Liberal Arts Colleges in the United States. Additionally, *Forbes* magazine chose Williams as the best undergraduate institution in the United States in its 2014 publication of "America's Top Colleges."

Field Park, at the junction of Routes 7 and 2, is what's primarily remaining of the town green, although the wide span of grass between the sidewalk and street and big front lawns from the park to the downtown (about a ten-minute walk) hint at a once truly expansive town green. Consider this passage from "Williamstown 1753–2003":

> The use of the wide street as a commons for cattle, hogs and geese compelled the abutting owners to protect themselves with fences. Almost every year for seventy-five years, there was agitation in town meetings over the issue of permitting the use of common for pasture. Finally, about 1876, pasturage was forbidden; the fences were removed—with the help of anonymous college students who pulled the last fences out on 1878 and made a huge bonfire of them; Cyrus W. Field and the Village

**The 1753 House—a 1953 historical replica of a regulation settler's home—is located in the middle of Field Park, Williamstown's town green.**

Improvement Society created Field Park at the Square and Main Street began to resemble its modern self.

Field and the Village Improvement Society's vision serves quite well to this very day, as today a meticulously well-landscaped town green holds events and ceremonies like a Memorial Day observance and the annual Carol Sing in December at the 1753 House on the green (a 1953 historical replica of a regulation settler's home in the Berkshires in 1753).

Here's a little bit about Williamstown's history: Originally called West Hoosac when first settled in 1749, Williamstown officially became incorporated in 1765. With dairy farming, sheep herding, and wool production in the agricultural days, and textiles and twine dominating the industrial age, it was the opening of the railroad that ultimately changed the commerce element of Williamstown into a tourist town, according to "A History of Williamstown" on the Town of Williamstown, Massachusetts, website (williamstown.ws/?page_id=161). The setting is beyond appealing, with a classic "Main Street USA" look and a mountainous setting. The Appalachian Trail skirts the town twice, and the highest point in town is at 3,320 feet above sea level, just 0.2 mile west of the summit of Mount Greylock.

While the remaining town green at Field Park looks great and has some historical value given its 1878 inception as a common, the best way to appreciate historic Williamstown is by combining the town green experience with a self-guided tour of downtown and also nearby South Williamstown. This way you can get a taste of town-green life even if the whole common is no longer intact. Here is a recommended self-guided tour, courtesy of the Williamstown Historical Museum (definitely worth exploring, too!) at 1095 Main Street (413-458-2160): www.williamstownhistoricalmuseum.org/programs-events/walking-tour/.

# WINCHENDON

Known as the Old Centre, the Winchendon town green exhibits deep historic roots that, to this very day, retain a wonderful sense of preservation. As the original town center of a town first settled by Europeans (mostly of English and Scottish descent) in 1752 and incorporated in 1764, the town green accommodated training grounds, the oldest burial ground, the first meetinghouse location, and a bevy of social activities within its parklike setting. It is no surprise that Winchendon has designated the area a "Winchendon Center Historic District" and that the National Register of Historic Places has designated it on its famous list. The town green is located on a hill—strategic for thwarting potential attacks from Native Americans on the early European settlers.

Today the 1950 First Congregational Church, Day House (the site of the first town meeting), and many fine old homes grace the town green area. Eventually the town center moved down the hill, as Winchendon's role as a manufacturing town—including woodworking, metals, and woolen mill sites—benefited from the Millers River presence in its newer location. Winchendon produced so many wooden shingles that it was nicknamed "Shingletown," according to John H. White in his excellent article, "A Brief History of Winchendon," on the Town of Winchendon's website at www.townofwinchendon.com/Pages/WinchendonMA_Webdocs/History1.

Winchendon's great manufacturing claim-to-fame, though, was as the biggest toy-manufacturing place in the world. Winchendon resident Morton Converse created Converse Toy & Woodware Company in late 1887 with a dedication to well-made toys that were

**Fall at the Winchendon town green during twilight offers a relaxing scenario.**

affordable to all until its closure in 1934. Some popular toys included Noah's Arks, doll furniture, kiddie riding racers, hobby horses, floor whirligigs, drums, wagon blocks, building blocks, pianos, trunks, ten pins, farm houses, and musical roller chimes, according to the "Converse" page on the All About Old Toys website (www.oldwoodtoys .com/converse.htm).

Within walking distance of the town common is Clyde, the toy rocking horse—built four times the normal size—that is displayed under a shelter!

# WINCHESTER

Just eight miles north of Boston, Winchester seems worlds away from the "Hub of the Universe" with seemingly some of the largest homes on the planet (with a high concentration of stunning Victorians), a waterfront setting on Mystic Lake, a beautiful quaint town center with enough locally owned stores to keep it interesting, and, of course, a wonderful town common. Following the true traditional New England spirit of a town common, it's a well-used space where people love to stroll, take lunch breaks, enjoy family picnics—or visit as part of time spent shopping and dining in the town center.

Purchased for seven thousand dollars by the town in 1867 from the former Converse Farm, the town common initially served as a scenic meeting place, but unfortunately fell into disrepair. The year 1875 served as a fortunate turning point, however, when the town allocated $750 to beautifying and maintaining the common by planting trees, adding a fountain, and, as we all know, recognizing the aesthetic importance of regularly mowing the lawn, according to Benjamin Eid in Winchester's Historic, Commemorative and Memorial Signs & Markers.

That 1875 turning point, however, took a turn for the worse. For many years the park commissioner, Charles Lane, kept the fountain stocked with goldfish of various sizes, but that came to an end when some rotten kids regularly threw rocks at the poor fish, according to Eid. Additionally, the town green fell repeatedly into disrepair and budget cuts dampened any hope of revitalizing this innately beautiful land. Fortunately, the Village Improvement Association and Rotary Club put pressure on the town to bring the town green back to its

**The Winchester town green is exceptionally cared for with great landscaping.**

original luster. History happily repeated itself with more trees planted, another fountain installed, and new grass planted, says Eid. The moral of this story is that sometimes all it takes is a few simple measures to restore a local treasure!

New Englanders love to recognize hard-working citizens and businesses, so it's no surprise that the renovation of the town common resulted in a plaque dedicated to the benefactors who donated to its improvement. It was placed in 1988, and since then the town green has been exceptionally well kept and utilized.

Events that take place on the Winchester town green include summer concerts on the common every Wednesday.

# WORCESTER

With virtually every blink of the eye, Worcester seems to be engaged in some sort of revitalization, and that's a good thing, seeing as it's the second-most populated city in New England at 182,000. With CitySquare in the works—a $565 million, twelve-acre, mixed-use development near Worcester City Hall—the development complements a solid core of nine colleges, art and science museums, and a symphony orchestra. There is no question that Worcester has evolved into a major player in the world of impressive New England cities.

Worcester, however, already showed urban greatness with a wonderful history that has been, in many areas, extremely well preserved. The City Hall Common—bounded by Main Street to the west, Franklin Street to the south, and Front Street to the north and east—serves as a wonderful reminder of Worcester's past and present, as well as its "solid rock" of the future. Modern-day visitors enjoy the 4.4-acre urban oasis with a summer concert "Out to Lunch" series, farmers' markets, winter ice skating at the Worcester Common Oval, and the Annual Festival of Lights celebration with "a visit from Santa Claus, children's choral performances, a holiday tree lighting, concessions, free hot cocoa, horse-drawn wagon rides and public ice skating," according to the events page of the City of Worcester's website (www.worcesterma.gov/calendar/festival-lights).

Two noteworthy monuments reside on the Worcester Common. The Colonel Timothy Bigelow monument, near the center of the common, honors Worcester soldiers of the Sixth Massachusetts Regiment "on their way to the front at the outbreak of the Civil War, (who) were being attacked by the Baltimore mob," according

**The Worcester Common offers one of the best urban green experiences in Massachusetts.**

to Zelotes W. Coomb's superb article on the Worcester Common at www.worcesterma.gov/city-clerk/history/general/worcester-common. The Soldiers Monument is a memorial to Civil War heroes, dedicated on July 15, 1874. Other important dedication sites include one of former Massachusetts Senator George Frisbie Hoar, and the Burnside Memorial Fountain erected in 1918 and dedicated to a prominent Worcester lawyer.

The monuments, memorials, and open space that locals and visitors see today only hint at this area's amazing history.

Listed on the National Register of Historic Places, the current version of the Worcester Common goes back to the early 1700s. It started out as twenty acres but was reduced to under five, as various city developments occurred in the town's transformation from agricultural community to industrial giant. A meetinghouse served as the first public building erected on the City Common, built in 1719 and host of the first town meeting in 1722. Religious and civic endeavors took place at the meetinghouse. As with most town commons that evolve over time, the larger, more modern Old South Meeting House replaced the original building and is filled with significant US history—like on July 14, 1776, when Isaiah Thomas read the Declaration of Independence for the first time in New England from the building's front porch.

With a town hall built in 1824–1825 and the community evolving into a major city at the cusp of industrial dominance, the city tore the old building down, but not all was lost. One could argue that the best was yet to come in the city common area.

The City of Worcester website states that from "1825 until Mechanics Hall was opened, the Town Hall, with its 'upper' Town Hall which had the largest seating capacity of any room in Worcester, became the center of the civic as well as the political life of the town." Concerts, lectures, and assemblies took place. Guests included President John Quincy Adams, Henry Clay, Charles Sumner, Daniel Webster, Father Matthew, Henry Wilson,, P. T. Barnum, Edward Everett, and in 1857 John Brown, according to the City of Worcester website. These early day statesmen and celebrities "spoke on behalf of themselves or some movement of the day," according to the City's website.

History was made over and over in Worcester during the mid-1800s, as the City website states:

The first meeting of the Free Soil Party was held on June 18, 1848. Eli Thayer of Worcester, in 1854 made the first public announcement of his plan to protest against the Kansas–Nebraska

Act which was the beginning of the movement that saved Kansas from being a Slave State. July 20, 1854, the Republican Party of Massachusetts was organized here. From 1857 Mechanics Hall with its much larger accommodations became the Forum of Worcester, and the use of Upper Town Hall declined so that in 1866 it was finally closed.

In 1730 about an acre of land on the easterly end of the Common was set apart for a burying ground and as such was the principal cemetery of Worcester until 1795. The lot, enclosed by a stone wall, extended to a point near the present Soldier's Monument, then to about where the Timothy Bigelow Monument stands. For some reason it was not square but more like a keystone in shape. As a result of the neglect, the burial ground gradually became an eyesore and in 1854, the city had a plan made of the graves and the inscriptions copied from the headstones. The headstones were then laid flat on the graves and the whole plot covered with a foot of earth and leveled off.

Other significant city common elements included a 1723 town pound that for one hundred years took care of stray animals in town; a burial ground dating back to 1730 in use until 1824; an 1840 school brick house; a gun house, Hearse House, and the Hook and Ladder House; and a show ground for cattle and other shows from 1819 to 1854.

The common served, to no surprise, as a training or muster field starting in 1746, according to the City website, "at the threat of a French invasion, a whole military company was formed, drilled and equipped ready to march from this field." The Revolutionary period created the greatest city-common military participation, first with more than three thousand men from all parts of the country gathered on August 22, 1774, without arms on the Common. The same year saw six thousand men leaving "the Common to aid the Boston Patriots when word came of the seizure of a quantity of ammunition in Somerville by the British. This expedition reached Shrewsbury before it was found that its services were not needed. However, from then on a company of Minute Men was organized under Captain Timothy Bigelow and, armed with muskets and cannon, drilled daily on the common. Their call came April 19, 1775, and although they took no part in the battles of Lexington and Concord, they became a part of General Artemus Ward's forces at Cambridge."

Railroads played a major role in the mid-1800s, when tracks were constructed across the common so that new companies could use the terminals for the Norwich & Worcester and the Western Railroads. With traffic slowing to a crawl, however, the City of Worcester removed the rails in 1877 when Union Station at Washington Square provided a much-needed, more logical layout for railroads, states the city's website.

Like so many Massachusetts town greens, the Worcester City Common probably looks best in its modern-day form, with its neatly landscaped, well-paved walkways, and myriad events to create a nice community feeling. There is this myth that "back in the day" was always better, but railroads passing through the common, militia training grounds, an animal pound, and outdated buildings did not exactly always create a picturesque "Camelot." Not that Worcester is Camelot today, but the current city common serves as a reminder that respect to history while intuitively adjusting to residents' needs today (like finding open-space relief from city congestion and other stresses) results in the best of both worlds. The Worcester Common is just that: a truly great urban Massachusetts city green. 🌿

# WRENTHAM

Driving into Wrentham center is like coming home—even if you don't live there—and the welcoming mat is in the form of a beautiful two-acre common with a gazebo (built in 1974 by members of the Wrentham Jaycees who worked on weekends and early evenings to create a Bicentennial bandstand to celebrate the country's two hundredth birthday), benches, paved walkways, and plenty of trees for shade. For some reason the town green feels like more than two acres, perhaps because every step of the way seemingly brings something special to the senses. Look one way and you see the ultimate "small town USA" with an independently owned hardware store, diner, ice-cream stand, flower shop, and more mom-and-pop gems. Look at another side of the common and you'll see the magnificent Proctor House Inn that has been beautifully restored to its 1861 Second Empire French Victorian luster. Set your sights in another direction and you'll see the magnificent, towering Original Congregational Church of Wrentham—a Greek Revival structure built in 1834 featuring a spectacular four-stage tower. Then, look across the village green and you'll see the heart of New England with an oasis that has been designated for common use since 1685. It's also an exceptionally well-kept town green, clearly cared for, nurtured, and respected as a historical and modern-day treasure.

Gail Huff, a well-known local journalist best known as a superb reporter at WCVB-TV Channel 5 in Boston from 1993–2012, lived in Wrentham with husband—former Massachusetts Senator Scott Brown—and family for many years. She has nothing but overwhelm-

The Original Congregational Church of Wrentham is located right across the street from the welcoming Wrentham town green.

ingly special memories when thinking about the Wrentham town common.

Scott and I raised our children in Wrentham. During the twenty-five years that we lived there, the town's idyllic common served as a backdrop for so many wonderful times. We attended the Sunday night Concerts in the Common and it was there that our daughter Ayla sang for the first time in public. At seven years old she sang an Elvis song with an oldies band called The

Reminisants, and years later she would shoot one of her first music videos in the Common after becoming a finalist on *American Idol*. Scott and the girls spent many days standing out in the Common with campaign signs during his twelve campaigns!

We never missed Wrentham Day when the Girl Scouts would be called in to volunteer. Scott was with the Lions Club and they'd put out one of the world's biggest banana splits for the kids to gobble up! Santa always met the townspeople at the Common on the Sunday after Thanksgiving. He rode in on a fire engine and listened to every child's deepest Christmas wishes before being whisked away to the North Pole. It was one of the few public Commons that still allowed displaying of the Crèche. To the children's delight, haphazardly strewn Christmas lights sparkled through many a nor'easter on Wrentham's town common. There were also solemn times, when sharing grief made the pain easier to bear. We cried together in the Common after the attacks of September 11. And we gathered for ceremonies that marked the lives of brave soldiers who never made it back home. We waved American flags and sang the National Anthem in a patriotic show of unity. There is nothing common about the Wrentham Common. Gathered souls at the little white gazebo, we'd share joy and sorrow—often wishing time could just stand still here.

Although Wrentham is a semirural town with a great dedication to historical preservation, it's interesting to note that just over a mile down the road is the Wrentham Premium Outlets. This modern shopping center brings in visitors from all over the world. If only they knew that the town green is just up the road—many of their expectations of the "real New England" would be fully realized!

The Sunday night Concerts on the Commons in summer, Arts in the Park in May, and the tree-lighting ceremony on the first Sunday of December make for some truly special times at the sleepy but vibrant Wrentham town common.

# Selected Bibliography

All About Old Toys. "Winchendon, Converse," www.oldwoodtoys
.com/converse.htm.

Authelet, Jack. "A Town, Its People, Their Common," 2012 Foxborough Annual Report. Foxborough MA Patch, http://patch.com/
massachusetts/foxborough/a-town-its-people-their-common-a
-foxborough-dedication.

Barber, John Warner. "Historical Collections Relating to the History
and Antiquities of Every Town in Massachusetts with Geographical Descriptions," Warren Lazell: 1848. http://history.rays-place
.com/ma/worcester/sturbridge.htm. Worcester, MA.

Baumgarten, Ron. "All Not So Quiet Along the Potomac," http://
dclawyeronthecivilwar.blogspot.com/2013/08/new-england-civil
-war-monuments.html.

Beaman, G. H. "A Brief History of Princeton," Town of Princeton,
Massachusetts, www.town.princeton.ma.us/Pages/PrincetonMA_
WebDocs/brief.

Bedford Free Public Library. www.bedfordlibrary.net.

Bedford Historical Society. www.bedfordmahistory.org/.

Belchertown, Massachusetts. "Profile of Belchertown," www.belchertown
.org/residents/general_town_info/profile_of_belchertown.php.

Bertrand Nancy. "History:," Wakefield, MA Patch, February 22, 2011.
http://patch.com/massachusetts/wakefield/history-wakefields
-soldiers-and-sailors-monument.

Betances Yadira. "Lawrence's Historic Campagnone Common Slated
for Renovations," *Lawrence Eagle Tribune*, January 28, 2012.

Bodanza, Mark. "'First Church has rich history," Leominster Champion online newspaper, January 23, 2009.

Boston Discovery Guide—Boston Public Garden. www.boston
-discovery-guide.com/boston-public-garden.html.

Brinkley, Rob. "All Is Calm," *New England Home* magazine, April 30,
2012.

Brookfield Apple County Fair. http://applecountryfair.com.

Cambridge Common. "Cambridge Historical Tours," http://cambridge historicaltours.org/about-us/sites/cambridge-common/.

Cape Cod Neighborhoods. "The Historic Eastham Windmill," www .capecodneighborhoods.com/blog/the-historic-eastham-windmill .html.

Carpenter, Edward Wilson and Charles Frederick Morehouse. "The History of the Town of Amherst, Massachusetts," Press of Carpenter & Morehouse: Amherst, MA, 1896.

Caswell, Lilley Brewer and Fred Wilder Cross. The history of the town of Royalston, Massachusetts. The Town of Royalston, 1917.

City of Boston. "Boston Common," www.cityofboston.gov/freedom trail/bostoncommon.asp.

City of Boston. "Bowdoin/Geneva," www.cityofboston.gov/images_ documents/Bowdoin_tcm3-25311.pdf.

City of Cambridge. "Cambridge Common," www.cambridgema.gov/ cdd/parks/parksinfo/parks/cambridgecommon.aspx.

City of Lawrence. "Campagnone Common," www.cityoflawrence.com/ campagnone-common.aspx.

City of Worcester. "City Hall Common (Paul V. Mullaney Plaza)," www .worcesterma.gov/dpw/parks-rec/city-parks/city-hall-common.

City of Worcester. "City Hall Common," www.worcesterma.gov/ dpw/parks-rec/city-parks/city-hall-common.

Commonwealth of Massachusetts. "National Register of Historic Places nomination for Barre Common Historic District." Date not found.

Commonwealth of Massachusetts. "National Register of Historic Places nomination for Brookfield Common Historic District," Feb. 23, 1990.

Commonwealth of Massachusetts. "National Register of Historic Places nomination for (Waltham) Central Square Historic District," August 1986.

Commonwealth of Massachusetts. "National Register of Historic Places nomination for Dedham Village Historic District," July 12, 2006.

Commonwealth of Massachusetts. "National Register of Historic Places nomination for East Bridgewater Common Historic District." Date not found.

Commonwealth of Massachusetts. "National Register of Historic Places nomination for Eastham Center Historic District," April 12, 1999.

Commonwealth of Massachusetts. "National Register of Historic Places nomination for Falmouth Village Green Historic District," September 1995.

Commonwealth of Massachusetts. "National Register of Historic Places nomination for Franklin Common Historic District," Feb. 14, 2005.

Commonwealth of Massachusetts. "National Register of Historic Places nomination for Grafton Common Historic District," March 1980.

Commonwealth of Massachusetts. "National Register of Historic Places nomination for Greenfield Main Street Historic District." 1984.

Commonwealth of Massachusetts. "National Register of Historic Places nomination for Harvard Common Historic District," June 1993.

Commonwealth of Massachusetts. "National Register of Historic Places nomination for Longmeadow Historic District." No date found.

Commonwealth of Massachusetts. "National Register of Historic Places nomination for Natick Center Historic District," Dec. 16, 1977.

Commonwealth of Massachusetts. "National Register of Historic Places nomination for New Salem Center Historic District," April 30, 1977.

Commonwealth of Massachusetts. "National Register of Historic Places nomination for Park Square Historic District." No date found.

Commonwealth of Massachusetts. "National Register of Historic Places nomination for Sterling Center Historic District." No date found.

Commonwealth of Massachusetts. "National Register of Historic Places nomination for Sutton Center Historic District," April 12, 2001.

Commonwealth of Massachusetts. "National Register of Historic Places nomination for Waltham Central Square Historic District," August 1986.

Cook, Edward M. "… and then there's Meeting House Hill …" *Dorchester Reporter*, Jan. 8, 2014.

Coombs, Zelotes W. "Worcester and Worcester Common." City of Worcester, MA. www.worcesterma.gov/city-clerk/history/general/worcester-common.

Copeland, Jennie F. "Mansfield's History," Town of Mansfield, MA, www.mansfieldma.com/html/history.html.

Cultural Land Foundation. "Pittsfield Park Square," https://tclf.org/landscapes/pittsfield-park-square.

Cushing, John D. "Town Commons of New England 1640–1840" Historic New England, www.historicnewengland.org/preservation/your-older-or-historic-home/articles/pdf86.pdf.

Daggett, John. "A Sketch of the History of Attleborough: From Its Settlement to the Division," Press of S. Usher, 1894.

Doerfler, Andrew. "Mansfield selectmen vote against signs for South Common event, saying they promote sponsor," *Attleboro Sun Chronicle*, Sept. 10, 2015.

Eid, Benjamin. "Winchester's Historic, Commemorative and Memorial Signs & Markers," August 26, 2013.

Emerald Necklace. www.emeraldnecklace.org/park-overview/park-map/.

Emily Dickinson Museum. "The Town and the Times," www.emilydickinsonmuseum.org/town_and_times.

First Church Ipswich. http://firstchurchipswich.org/.

First Church and Parish Dedham. "375 Years of History in Short," www.dedhamuu.org/#!our-history/cs4a/Dedham%20Decision/c21th.

First Parish Dorchester. "Social Action," www.firstparishdorchester.

First Parish of Bedford. www.uubedford.org/about-us/heritage.html.

First Parish of Groton. http://uugroton.org/.

Freedom's Way Bedford, MA. "Path of the Patriot," www.freedoms way.org/towns/bedford/bedford.html.

Freedom's Way Heritage Association. "Fitchburg Reconnaissance Report," Massachusetts Department of Conservation and Recreation, June 2006.

The Future Is Not Today blog. "Putterin around Petersham," http://nomadwillie.blogspot.com/2013/12/putterin-around-petersham -ma.html.

Garfield, Curtis. "Sudbury, 1890–1989, 100 years in the Life of a Town," *Porcupine Enterprises*, 1999. Sudbury, MA.

Goldstein, Karin. "The Training Green: From Training to Temperance to Art," Plymouth Patch, Oct. 2, 2011. http://patch.com/ massachusetts/plymouth/the-training-green-from-traning-to -temperance-to-art.

"Greenfield Reconnaissance Report," Massachusetts Department of Conservation and Recreation, June 2009.

Hardwick Community Fair. www.hardwickfair.com/.

Historic Buildings of Massachusetts. "Andrew-Safford House (1818)," http://mass.historicbuildingsct.com/?p=2867.

Historic Deerfield. www.historic-deerfield.org/.

Historic District Commission–Town of Petersham Massachusetts. http://townofpetersham.weebly.com/historic-district-commission.html.

Ipswich Museum. www.ipswichmuseum.org.

Ipswich Visitor Center. www.ipswichvisitorcenter.org.

Johnny Appleseed Craft Beer Festival. www.johnnyappleseedbeerfest .com.

Johnny Appleseed Festival website. http://leominsterevents.com/ event/johnny-appleseed-festival.

Kleeberg. "Gazebo," www.kleeberg.com/portfolio/gazebo.php.

"Lawrence Reconnaissance Report." Massachusetts Historical Commission, 1997.

Leominster, Massachusetts. "Winter Stroll and Mayor's Tree Lighting Ceremony," http://leominsterevents.com/event/winter-stroll-and -mayors-tree-lighting-ceremony/.

Levine, David. "A Secret Jewel: Barre, MA," History Stands Still, http://bandstands.blogspot.com/2009/04/barre-ma.html. Information furnished by Linda J. Payne, Library Assistant. Woods Memorial Library, Barre.

Levine, David. "A Secret Jewel: Belchertown, MA." History Stands Still, http://bandstands.blogspot.com/2009/04/belchertown-ma.html. Information furnished by Doris Dickinson, Curator Stone House Museum, Belchertown.

Levine, David. "A Secret Jewel: Freetown, MA." History Stands Still, http://bandstands.blogspot.com/search/label/Freetown%20MA. Information furnished by Melanie Doddskoff, Curator, Freetown Historical Society.

Levine, David. "A Secret Jewel: Walpole, MA." History Stands Still, http://bandstands.blogspot.com/search/label/Walpole%20MA. Information furnished by Elizabeth M. Cottrell, Member, Walpole Historical Commission and Historical Society.

Lewis J. Paul. "The Historical Development of Cambridge Common," Cambridge Historical Society, 1974.

Massachusetts Historical Society. "First Parish Church of Dorchester Records 1636–1981, Guide to the Collection," www.masshist.org/collection-guides/view/fa0041.

MassHome. "Notable Events in Massachusetts History," www.masshome.com/events.html.

MassLive.com. "West Brookfield gets $100,000 grant to restore Rice Memorial Fountain," *The Republican*, www.masslive.com/living/index.ssf/2013/03/west_brookfield_gets_100000_grant_to_restore_rice_memorial_fountain.html.

Natick, Massachusetts. "Town Common," http://natickma.gov/1126/Town-Common.

Neighborhood Scout. "Town Center Sudbury, MA Neighborhood Profile," www.neighborhoodscout.com/ma/sudbury/town-center/.

North Andover Historical Society. www.northandoverhistoricalsociety.org/.

"North Andover Reconnaissance Report," Massachusetts Department of Conservation and Recreation, Essex National Heritage Commission, May 2005.

Old Colony History Museum. www.oldcolonyhistorymuseum.org/society/history.htm.

O'Malley, Patricia Trainor. "Bradford: The End of an Era," Arcadia Publishing, 1996. Mount Pleasant SC.

Phaneuf, Wayne. "Springfield's 375th: City monuments honor those who answered the call of duty," MassLive, www.masslive.com/history/index.ssf/2011/05/springfields_375th_city_monuments_honor_those_who_answered_the_call.html, May 29, 2011.

Provencher, Shaun. "Common Wealth: The Past and Future of Town Commons," Terra Firm, Massachusetts Department of Conservation and Recreation, 2008.

"Public Space: Common Institutions," Dorr, Holland and Company, 1839, www.americancenturies.mass.edu/turns/view.jsp?itemid=12874&subthemeid=9.

National Park Service. "Concord Monument Square in the Concord Monument Square–Lexington," www.nps.gov/nr/travel/massachusetts_conservation/concord_monument_square.html.

National Park Service. "Dana Common," www.nps.gov/nr/travel/massachusetts_conservation/dana_common.html.

National Park Service. "Shirley Center Historic District," www.nps.gov/nr/travel/massachusetts_conservation/shirley_center.html).

Roxbury Land Trust. "History," www.roxburylandtrustorg.

Roylaston Historical. www.royalstonhistorical.org/.

Salem Common Neighborhood Association. "History of the Salem Common District," www.salemcommon.org/history/.

Salem, Massachusetts—the Comprehensive Salem Guide. "Washington Square Historic District," www.salemweb.com/guide/arch/wdistrict.php.

"Self-Guided Tours of Williamstown." Williamstown Historical Museum, www.williamstownhistoricalmuseum.org/programs-events/walking-tour/.

Spence, Benjamin A. "Law and Order in Colonial Bridgewater, Massachusetts, with Special Emphasis on Its South Parish/Precinct," 2012. http://bit.ly/1K6nh6z.

Springfield Massachusetts. Revolutionary Day. www.revolutionaryday .com/usroute20/springfield/default.htm.

Sterling Historical Commission. "A Brief History of Sterling," 1991.

Sterling Historical Society. www.sterlinghistorical.org/.

"Sturbridge Reconnaissance Report." Massachusetts Heritage Landscape Program, Massachusetts Department of Conservation and Recreation, June 2007.

Tour Lexington. www.libertyride.us/historic.html.

Tour Lexington, Massachusetts. "Historic Sites and Museums," www .libertyride.us/historic.html.

Town of New Salem Old Home Day Committee. www.newsalem -massachusetts.org/committeesboards/oldhomedaycommittee .html.

Town of Sterling. "Town History," www.sterling-ma.gov/home/pages/ town-history.

Town of Sudbury. "A Brief History of the Town of Sudbury, MA, U. S. A.," https://www.sudbury.ma.us/services/seniorcenter/custom/ hal/sudbury.htm#Hist1.

Town of Sudbury. "King Philip's War and The Sudbury Fight." https:// sudbury.ma.us/services/seniorcenter/custom/hal/kpwar.htm.

Town of Sudbury. "Sudbury's Historic Districts," https://www.sudbury .ma.us/committees/historicdistricts/custom/historicdistricts.asp.

Town of Williamstown, Massachusetts. "History of Williamstown," http://williamstown.ws/?page_id=161.

Trust for Architectural Easements. http://architecturaltrust.org/ easements/about-the-trust/trust-protected-communities/historic -districts-in-massachusetts/cohasset-common-historic-district/.

"Wakefield Preservation Plan," Town of Wakefield, Massachusetts, 2001.

Waymarking.com. "New Salem Common Historic District–New Salem," www.waymarking.com/waymarks/WMHN0G_New_ Salem_Common_Historic_District_New_Salem_MA.

Waymarking.com. "Norwood Town Common–Norwood, MA," www.waymarking.com/waymarks/WM7MKV_Norwood_Town _Common_Norwood_MA.

West Boylston Massachusetts Historical Society. www.wbhistory.org/.

West Brookfield Historical Commission. http://westbrookfield.org/.

West Brookfield Historical Commission. "Walking Tour," http://west brookfield.org/walking-tour/.

Weston Historical Commission. http://westhistcomm.org/.

Weston Historical Society. http://westonhistory.org/.

White, John H. "A Brief History of Winchendon," Town of Winchendon, MA, www.townofwinchendon.com/Pages/Winchendon MA_Webdocs/History1.

# About the Author

**Eric Hurwitz** writes straight from the heart on New England travel for his readers on VisitingNewEngland.com. A lifelong New Englander inspired on a daily basis by the six-state region, Hurwitz has covered many aspects of New England travel since 2001, but with a particular interest in sharing hidden destinations, attractions, and restaurants with his audience. Through the years, media and online informational outlets like *USA Today*, *Woman's World*, the Maine Office of Tourism, BusinessInsider.com, eHow.com, and Wikipedia.com have referenced select VisitingNewEngland.com articles. Hurwitz holds a bachelor's degree in journalism from Suffolk University in Boston and spent twenty-plus years as a reporter, assistant editor, and public affairs specialist in the public and private sectors before starting his work of love, VisitingNewEngland.com.